BECOMING *her*

THE SOVEREIGN SOFT LIFE OF A KINGDOM WOMAN

WRITTEN BY
KAREN Y. MOORE

BECOMING HER

The Sovereign Soft Life of a Kingdom Woman

KAREN Y. MOORE

Copyright © 2026 by Karen Y. Moore

All rights reserved.

No part of this book may be reproduced, distributed, or transmitted in any form or by any means, including photocopying, recording, or other electronic or mechanical methods, without the prior written permission of the author, except in the case of brief quotations embodied in critical reviews and certain other noncommercial uses permitted by copyright law.

For permission requests, contact:
www.karenymoore.com

Published by KYM Lifestyle
Las Vegas, Nevada
Cover design by Karen Y. Moore
Interior design and formatting by TL Mason

First Edition: February 2026
ISBN: 978-1-7335168-8-4

DEDICATION

To every woman who has spent years being
"the strong one"

while her own life waited in the wings.

To the 57-year-old who thinks she's too late.

To the 42-year-old who's just realizing she's been living
everyone else's life.

To the caregiver who forgot she has a body.

To the widow still holding everyone else's center.

To the entrepreneur burning out in a business that
consumes her.

To the mother whose children are grown and who's
asking, "Now what?"

To the woman in her 60s, 70s, 80s who's been told her
season is over.

To the survivor who made it through but doesn't know
how to actually live.

To the woman staring in the mirror wondering
where she went.

This is your permission slip.

You are not too late. You are exactly on time.

And to Benjamin—

By choosing myself, I didn't lose you.

I found us both.

ACKNOWLEDGEMENTS

This book would not exist without the grace of God and the people He placed in my path during my most difficult season—and my season of becoming.

To my son, Benjamin: You are woven into every page of this story, even when you're not named. By choosing myself, I didn't lose you—I found us both. Thank you for relocating to Las Vegas and giving us the gift of proximity again. Our first Thanksgiving together since 2011, our first Christmas together since 2016—these are the miracles that remind me why I chose to emerge. You are my legacy, my joy, and proof that choosing yourself can save your family. I'm so proud of the man you've become. I love you.

To Traci Wade: Sister-friend, you have been my steady ground when the world felt unstable. You've held space for my grief, celebrated my small wins, and reminded me—over and over—that I was not too late. Thank you for seeing the woman I was becoming even when I couldn't see her yet. Your friendship is one of the greatest blessings of my life.

To Carolyn Tardd: Thank you for being my rock, for listening without judgment, and for showing up with steady love when I needed it most. Your friendship is priceless, and your presence in my life has been a gift I treasure deeply.

To Beverly Floyd: Your wisdom has shaped me in ways I'm still discovering. Thank you for speaking truth with love, for challenging me when I needed it, and for modeling what it looks like to live with both strength and grace. You've been a guide, a mentor, and a mirror showing me what's possible. I am grateful.

To Hector and Denise: You are family in the truest sense—not by blood, but by choice, loyalty, and love. Thank you for being my extended family when I needed one most. Thank you for your support, your laughter, your presence, and for reminding me that family isn't just who you're born to—it's who shows up. You are deeply loved and deeply appreciated.

To the women who will read this book: You are the reason I wrote it. If my story gives you permission to choose yourself, to honor your temple, to build the Sovereign Soft Life—then every hard moment, every tear, every doubt was worth it. You are not too late. You are exactly on time.

And to James: Though you're no longer here, your love shaped me. The sixteen years we had together taught me what devotion looks like. I carry you with me in every step of this becoming. Until we meet again.

Above all, I thank God—for sparing my life three times, for leading me to the desert, for teaching me what it means to be a daughter of the King, and for showing me that my body is a temple, rest is holy, and choosing myself is sacred stewardship.

Soli Deo Gloria.

TABLE OF CONTENTS

HOW TO USE THIS BOOK 1

INTRODUCTION: The Cocoon Is Breaking Open 3

PART I: THE AWAKENING 9

   Chapter 1: The Cocoon of Survival 11

   Chapter 2: The Three Deaths & The Mandate for Life 21

   Chapter 3: The Sacred Exit & The Move to Vegas 35

PART II: KINGDOM EMBODIMENT *(The Temple)* 45

   Chapter 4: Your Body as Sanctuary, Not Sacrifice 47

   Chapter 5: The Warrior Archetype & Protective Leadership 59

   Chapter 6: The Proverbs 31 Woman Reimagined 73

PART III: THE SOVEREIGN SOFT LIFE *(The Framework)* 87

   Chapter 7: Defining the Sovereign Soft Life 89

   Chapter 8: The P.R.I.V.É. Philosophy 101

   Chapter 9: Sabbath as Architecture 113

   Chapter 10: Kingdom Business & The Laptop Lifestyle 127

PART IV: THE 90-DAY EMERGENCE *(The Path Forward)* 143

   Chapter 11: The 90-Day Metamorphosis 145

CONCLUSION: THE INVITATION TO MEET HER 183

BONUS SECTION: RESOURCES FOR YOUR BECOMING 200

ABOUT THE AUTHOR 253

HOW TO USE THIS BOOK

*"In their hearts humans plan their course,
but the LORD establishes their steps."*

~Proverbs 16:9

This book is structured in four parts, but you don't have to read it linearly.

- If you're in survival mode right now → Start with Part I
- If you're struggling with your body → Start with Chapter 4
- If you need practical steps NOW → Jump to Part IV
- If you're designing a business → Start with Part III

Each chapter includes:

- The Story (real, lived experience)
- The Teaching (biblical wisdom + practical application)
- The Application (reflection questions and exercises)

Keep a journal nearby. The questions aren't rhetorical—they're invitations.

You are not starting over late in life.

You are starting as yourself, for the very first time.

INTRODUCTION:
The Cocoon Is Breaking Open

"Therefore, if anyone is in Christ, the new creation has come: The old has gone, the new is here!"

~2 Corinthians 5:17

The Cocoon Is Breaking Open

There is a specific kind of silence that follows sixteen years of noise. For nearly two decades, my life was a masterclass in endurance. I was the strong one. I was the one who held the center while everyone else's world spun. I was the woman who walked through the valley of the shadow of death—not once, but three times—battling sepsis and surviving what should have killed me.

I have been a daughter, a devoted wife to James, a mother, and a primary caregiver. I have been a survivor. But in all those roles, I realized something profound at the age of 57:

I had become a sacrifice, but I had never been a sanctuary for myself.

For years, I believed that my strength was measured by how much I could carry for others. I wore my exhaustion like a badge of devotion, unaware that I was slowly disappearing behind the needs of everyone else. I was "Postponed Karen"—the woman whose dreams, health, and very identity were on permanent mute while I held the line for everyone else.

On August 27, 2024, something broke.

My mother fell from her wheelchair. I waited forty-five minutes for help. And when a hospital social worker looked me in the eye and said, "You need help," I finally heard what I'd been too afraid to admit.

That was the day I chose myself. It wasn't abandonment—it was stewardship. I placed my mother in skilled nursing care. And for the first time in my adult life, I looked in the mirror and decided to meet the woman staring back at me.

I drove from Savannah to Denver, then on to Las Vegas. When I crossed the city limits on November 20th, a weight I didn't know I was carrying dissolved into the desert air. I wasn't just changing cities. I was emerging.

If you're reading this, you might be the woman I used to be. The "strong one" who's been waiting in the wings while your own life played out as someone else's supporting role. You may be navigating the wreckage of loss, the depletion of caregiving, or the quiet desperation of a dream deferred.

I am here to tell you: **The cocoon is breaking open.**

What This Book Is

This book is not another hustle manual. It's not a prescription for performing more strength while secretly starving. This is a roadmap to the **Sovereign Soft Life**—a Kingdom-aligned existence where your body is a temple, not a tool. Where rest is holy. Where your business serves your life instead of consuming it.

I'm not teaching theory. I'm teaching from lived transformation. I'm discovering who I become when I'm completely healed, fully embodied, and living from overflow instead of depletion. And I'm inviting you to discover it with me.

This is a book about **embodiment**—fully inhabiting your transformed self. It's about moving from performing strength to being strong. From survival mode to sovereignty. From depletion to the Sovereign Soft Life.

Who This Book Is For

This book is for you if:

- You've spent years being "the strong one" while your own dreams waited in the wings
- You're navigating reinvention after loss, caregiving, or trauma
- You're exhausted by businesses or careers that consume you instead of serving you
- You're ready to treat your body as a temple, not a tool for serving others
- You're a woman of faith seeking to build Kingdom-aligned work that honors Sabbath rest
- You're in your second act (40s, 50s, 60s, 70s+) and ready to finally choose yourself
- You're tired of performing strength and ready to embody sovereignty
- You want to build a life that doesn't require hardness to survive

This is for the woman who knows, deep down, that choosing herself isn't selfish—it's sacred stewardship.

Who This Book Is NOT For

This book is not for you if:

- You're looking for quick fixes or "5 easy steps to success"

- You want another hustle-harder business manual

- You're not willing to examine the weight you're carrying and release what's not yours

- You're seeking permission to avoid responsibility (this is about stewardship, not abandonment)

- You're uncomfortable with faith-based teaching rooted in Scripture

- You're not ready to honor rest, boundaries, and Sabbath as non-negotiable

- You want theory without application (this book requires you to do the work)

If you're looking for surface-level inspiration without transformation, this isn't your book. But if you're ready to emerge—messy middle and all—keep reading.

How to Use This Book

This book is structured in four parts, each building on the last:

Part I: The Awakening - Understanding where you are and how you got here. Honoring the postponed self and choosing the Sacred Exit.

Part II: Kingdom Embodiment - Learning to inhabit your body as sanctuary, reclaiming the Proverbs 31 woman as your model, and embodying protective leadership.

Part III: The Sovereign Soft Life - The frameworks that make sovereignty sustainable: removing unnecessary weight, honoring Sabbath as architecture, and building Kingdom businesses that serve your life.

Part IV: The 90-Day Emergence - Your practical roadmap for navigating the messy middle and stepping into your becoming.

Each chapter follows the same structure:

- **The Story** (mine or a composite of women I've worked with)
- **The Teaching** (biblical wisdom + practical application)
- **The Application** (reflection questions, exercises, practices)

You can read this book straight through, or you can focus on the part that's calling to you right now. If you're in the awakening stage, start with Part I. If you're ready for practical frameworks, jump to Part III. There's no wrong way to use this book—only YOUR way.

I recommend keeping a journal nearby. The reflection questions aren't rhetorical—they're invitations to meet yourself on the page.

You aren't starting over late in life. You are starting as yourself, for the very first time. We are going to stop performing strength and start embodying sovereignty.

The question I asked myself, and the one I now ask you, is this:

Who are you when you are no longer needed as a sacrifice, but chosen as a sanctuary?

Let's find out together.

In Part I, you'll witness the cocoon—the years of survival that required everything I had. In Part II, you'll learn what it means to finally inhabit this transformed body, to treat it as the temple it was always meant to be. In Part III, I'll show you how to build the Sovereign Soft Life—the frameworks that make sovereignty sustainable. And in Part IV, you'll receive your roadmap for the messy middle, because metamorphosis isn't linear, and grace is required for the journey.

This book isn't about arriving. It's about becoming. And becoming requires you to meet yourself exactly where you are—in the cocoon, in the breaking open, or in the first trembling moments of flight.

You are not too late. You are exactly on time.

PART I:
THE AWAKENING

"He gives strength to the weary and increases the power of the weak."
~Isaiah 40:29

(The Foundation of Becoming)

Chapter 1:
THE COCOON OF SURVIVAL

In the quiet of my new Las Vegas sanctuary, I often look back at the woman I was in November 2008. That was the month my mother moved into my Savannah home, bringing with her a walker, a lifetime of belongings, and a new rhythm that would reshape the next sixteen years of my life.

I remember the sound of her walker scraping across the hardwood floors at 3 AM. The way my calendar slowly filled with doctor's appointments instead of dreams. The subtle, creeping silence where my own desires used to live.

Six months later, the world stopped.

On May 5, 2009, I lost James. Transitioning from a wife to a widow while simultaneously serving as a full-time caregiver created a singular kind of pressure. My son, Benjamin, was two weeks from prom, four weeks from graduating high school. Instead of celebrating his milestones, I was planning a funeral and trying to hold our family together.

I didn't have the luxury of a slow, private grief. I had to be "Making-it-work Karen." I had to be the anchor for Benjamin and the strength for my mother. I had to keep moving because if I stopped, I was afraid everything would collapse.

For the next sixteen years, I inhabited the roles of "Grief-carrying Karen" and "Postponed Karen." I believed that my devotion was measured by my disappearance. If I was tired, I pushed harder. If I was sick, I ignored it. I was operating under the unspoken rule that so many Kingdom women follow: To be holy is to be hollowed out.

I wore my exhaustion like a badge. I carried it proudly to church, to family gatherings, to every conversation where someone would say, "I don't know how you do it." And I would smile and say, "God gives me strength," which was true—but incomplete. Because what I didn't say was that I was disappearing. That the woman I used to be was slowly being erased by the needs of everyone around me.

When you spend years as a tool for everyone else's survival, you eventually forget that you were designed to be a temple.

I'm telling you this not to make you feel sorry for me, but to give you permission to see yourself in my story. Because if you're reading this, you've likely lived some version of this cocoon. Maybe your cocoon was caregiving, like mine. Maybe it was a demanding career that left no room for your own life. Maybe it was a relationship where you became so small that you forgot you were supposed to take up space.

Whatever form it took, you know what it feels like to be the strong one while your own life waited in the wings.

So let me speak a truth into your life that took me nearly two decades to learn:

Trauma pauses identity. Grief puts whole parts of us on mute.

The sixteen years I spent caregiving were not a waste of my life. They were a season of extreme devotion and sacred sacrifice. However, there is a profound difference between a season and a permanent state of being. Many of us stay in the "survival cocoon" long after the season of survival has ended. We continue to perform the role of the "strong one" because we have forgotten how to be anything else.

If you are currently feeling the weight of a "postponed life," I want you to look at the roles you are performing. Are you holding the center because God called you to it for *this* moment, or are you holding it because you're afraid the world will fall apart if you let go?

Survival mode is a gift when you are in the thick of the storm. It numbs the pain so you can do the work. But once the storm has passed, staying in survival mode becomes a prison. It keeps you from the very "becoming" you were spared for.

So here's what I need you to hear:

It is time to distinguish between the roles you perform and the woman you are.

The roles were necessary for a season. The woman beneath them? She's been waiting to emerge.

The Teaching: Why We Postpone Ourselves

We often frame our self-neglect as a spiritual virtue. We tell ourselves that being "poured out" is the ultimate sign of a Kingdom woman. But there is a profound difference between being *poured out* and being *hollowed out*.

One is an act of overflow; the other is an act of depletion.

For sixteen years, I lived in the hollow. I believed that if I stopped holding the center, the world would stop spinning. This is the first lie of the "Survival Cocoon": the belief that our performance is the only thing standing between order and chaos.

When you inhabit the role of the "strong one," you inadvertently teach people how to use you, but you never teach them how to honor you. More importantly, you forget how to honor yourself.

I remember the first time someone called me "strong" after James died. It felt like praise. But over the years, "strong" became the only role I was allowed to play. If I cried, I was "losing it." If I admitted I was tired, I was "not coping well." So I learned to perform strength even when I was breaking.

And people—good people, loving people—learned to expect it. Not out of malice, but because I taught them that I could carry everything. I never taught them how to honor the woman beneath the weight.

This is what happens in the cocoon: We become so good at survival that people forget we were meant for more than endurance.

Trauma as a Pause Button

Trauma—whether it is the sudden shock of losing a spouse like James or the slow-motion trauma of long-term caregiving—acts as a pause button on the soul. When you are in the thick of a crisis, your brain shifts into "survival mode." In this state, your only job is to get through the next hour, the next medication dose, the next bill.

Your identity, your dreams, and your body's needs get shelved so you can function. The problem arises when the crisis ends, but you forget to hit "play."

You continue to live as if you are still in the emergency room long after you've returned home. You stay in the cocoon not because it's comfortable, but because it's familiar. You've forgotten who you are without a crisis to manage.

I lived this way for sixteen years. Even when my mother's health stabilized. Even when Benjamin built his own life. Even when there was space for me to breathe, I kept holding my breath. Because breathing felt like selfishness. Resting felt like abandonment. Choosing myself felt like betrayal.

But here's what I've learned:

The cocoon is meant to be temporary. Metamorphosis requires breaking open.

If you stay in the cocoon past its season, you don't become a butterfly. You become a woman who forgot she had wings.

The Sacred Act of Stopping

Society, and sometimes even our church cultures, will applaud you for your exhaustion. They will call you "selfless" while you are literally losing your self. They will give you awards for martyrdom while you're dying slowly in plain sight.

But I am here to tell you that stopping is a steward's work. If your body is a temple, you cannot treat it like a warehouse. If your life is a gift from God, you cannot spend it entirely as a sacrifice for everyone else's convenience.

This is the hard part: Choosing to stop doesn't feel like obedience. It feels like betrayal.

When I made the decision to place my mother in skilled nursing care in August 2024, I felt like I was failing her. Failing James. Failing the version of myself who had promised to "never give up."

But here's what I had to reckon with: I wasn't giving up. I was *giving her better care than I could provide alone* while simultaneously *choosing not to die trying*.

Because that's where I was headed. My body had already survived sepsis three times—the same illness that took James. My right great toe was amputated. I was in chronic pain. I couldn't lift her when she fell. I was one emergency away from becoming the patient instead of the caregiver.

God didn't spare me three times so I could die slowly in a cocoon of obligation. He spared me so I could LIVE. Fully. Embodied. Sovereign.

Stopping isn't quitting. Stopping is choosing to exit the emergency room now that the emergency is over. It's deciding that the woman God saw when He spared your life deserves to finally be met.

And if that feels selfish to you, let me reframe it:

Stewardship of self IS Kingdom work. You cannot pour from empty. You cannot lead from depletion. You cannot teach others to honor their bodies as temples if you're still treating yours like a tool.

Choosing to stop—choosing to exit the cocoon—is not an act of abandonment. It is an act of alignment. It is deciding that you are worthy of the same care, attention, and protection you've been giving everyone else.

When the Cocoon Becomes a Prison

There's a difference between being in a cocoon during active metamorphosis and being trapped in a cocoon long after the transformation was supposed to happen.

If you've been asking yourself, "When is it my turn?" for more than a year, you're likely past the season of necessary survival. You're in the prison of habitual self-abandonment.

The cocoon becomes a prison when:

- You can't remember the last time you made a decision based on what *you* wanted

- Your body is breaking down but you keep pushing through

- You resent the people you're serving but feel too guilty to stop

- You've been saying "someday" about your own dreams for years

- You feel more like a tool than a person

If any of these resonate, it's time to acknowledge: The season of survival is over. The season of becoming is here.

And becoming requires you to choose yourself—not once, but daily. Not as an act of selfishness, but as an act of sacred stewardship.

Because the woman you're becoming? She can't emerge if you're still performing the roles that kept you alive but never let you thrive.

The Application: Honoring the Woman You Carry

Leaving the cocoon requires an honest look at what you've been carrying. You cannot heal what you refuse to acknowledge. Before we move into the mechanics of your new life, we must honor the woman who got you here.

The Survival Audit

Take a moment with your journal. Look at the last few years of your life and answer these questions with radical honesty:

1. What roles have you been performing?
List them out—The Fixer, The Strong One, The Silent Supporter, The Caregiver, The Martyr, The Peacekeeper, The Problem-Solver.

Now, next to each role, write:
- How long have I been playing this role?
- Did I choose this, or did it choose me?
- What would happen if I stopped performing this role tomorrow?

The roles that scare you most to release are often the ones you need to examine most closely.

2. Where have you postponed yourself?
Is it your health? Your business ideas? Your rest? Your creativity? Your relationships? Your joy?

Identify the specific dreams, needs, or desires you put on "mute" so you could hold the center for others.

Write them down. Not to shame yourself, but to see clearly what's been waiting for you.

3. What is the cost of staying in the cocoon?

If nothing changes in the next twelve months, what will it cost your body, your peace, your spirit, and your legacy?

Be specific. "I'll be exhausted" is true but vague. Try: "My blood pressure will remain high. My chronic pain will worsen. I'll miss another year of actually living my life."

This isn't meant to scare you. It's meant to show you that staying in the cocoon has a price—and it's often higher than the price of emergence.

Journal Prompt: A Letter to "Survival You"

I want you to write a letter to the version of yourself that has been holding everything together. Do not write this from a place of frustration or judgment. Write it from a place of deep honor and gratitude.

Here's a template to get you started:

Dear [Your Name],

I see how hard you've worked to keep everyone safe. I see the sacrifices you made when the world was loud and the needs were great. I want to thank you for [list specific things you survived—the nights you stayed up, the pain you endured, the tears you swallowed, the dreams you deferred].

You did a beautiful job. You held the center when it felt like everything was falling apart. You kept going when most people would have quit.

But I need you to hear this: Your assignment as a sacrifice is complete. The emergency is over. The season has shifted.

I am taking the lead now. You can rest. It is safe for us to emerge. The woman we're becoming needs both of us—your strength AND your willingness to finally be soft.

Thank you for getting us here. Now, let me take us forward.

With love and honor,
[Your Name]

Affirmation for the Week

Place this somewhere you'll see it daily—on your mirror, your phone lock screen, your journal:

"My sixteen years (or my season of survival) were an act of devotion, not a waste of time. I am not behind; I am on time, and I am ready to be found."

Say it out loud every morning. Let it remind you: The cocoon is breaking open. Your becoming has already begun.

But knowing you've been in a cocoon is only the first step. Next, you must understand why you stayed so long—and what it took to finally choose life. Because for me, it took walking through death's door three times before I understood the mandate I'd been given. In the next chapter, I'll show you what survival taught me about truly living.

You are not too late. You are exactly on time.

Chapter 2:
THE THREE DEATHS & THE MANDATE FOR LIFE

"I have set before you life and death, blessings and curses. Now choose life, so that you and your children may live."

~Deuteronomy 30:19

In May 2009, I learned the name of my enemy: Sepsis. It was the thief that took James. I watched it move with a terrifying speed, transforming a vibrant life into a memory in what felt like a heartbeat. At the time, I thought that was my only encounter with that particular shadow. I thought my role was simply to survive the grief he left behind.

But seven years later, the shadow came for me.

Between 2016 and 2020, I walked through death's door three separate times. Each time, sepsis—the same illness that killed my husband—tried to take me too. Most people don't survive sepsis once. I've survived it three times.

And each time I was sent back, I learned something profound about what it means to truly live.

The Loss That Changed Everything: James, 2009

James was an executive chef Monday through Friday, but on weekends he pursued his true passion: photography. I owned a wedding and event planning business in Savannah, and James worked as my photographer. We were each other's best friend. If James wasn't at his Monday-Friday job, we were always together.

That first weekend of May 2009 was filled with so much love. We had our full schedule of meetings, weddings, and dinners with friends. James had been complaining about what we thought were allergy symptoms—watery eyes, runny nose—but we pushed through like we always did.

On Sunday, May 3rd, I officiated a wedding ceremony. During the ceremony, something extraordinary happened. I looked at James. Our eyes locked and tears started streaming down both our faces. This was the first time this had ever happened to me during a ceremony. I had to regain my composure to finish officiating.

I don't know why it happened. But perhaps our hearts knew what was coming.

We got home that evening. James took a shower and discovered he had a fever. I started alternating Tylenol and Advil every four hours. I begged him to let me take him to the emergency room immediately, but he insisted on waiting. "We'll see our primary care doctor first thing in the morning," he said.

His fever finally broke at 2:00 AM.

Two things have haunted me ever since: not insisting he go to the hospital that Sunday night, and the survivors' guilt that followed.

Monday Morning: When Everything Fell Apart

We got up around 6:00 AM to get ready for the doctor's office. Within an hour, James was vomiting and had diarrhea. He was so weak I had to call EMS to transport him.

In the emergency room, they told us he had an infection in his blood. James started losing feeling in his legs. He kept telling me he couldn't see. By 4:00 PM, they moved him to ICU.

Because they'd prepared a sterile environment, I couldn't go in with him. This devastated me. I kissed him on his forehead as they wheeled him away.

I never dreamed that would be our last kiss. The last time I would see him alive.

The attending physician made it clear that James's prognosis wasn't good. If he survived, he might have brain damage. The quality of his life would be severely diminished. It was going to be a long night, touch and go. He advised me to go home and rest, promising they'd call if anything changed.

I remember going home feeling scared, broken, and shattered. I took a shower and somehow fell asleep praying and hugging James's picture.

The call came around 2:00 AM on Tuesday, May 5th. James was slipping away.

I jumped out of bed and got dressed as fast as I could, praying the entire time for a miracle. When I got the call, I felt like someone had pulled the rug right out from under me while I was walking. I knew he was gone by the time I got to the hospital because I heard birds chirping.

Birds don't chirp at 3:00 AM.

My angel, my love, my soulmate—gone at 43 years old.

I didn't learn the cause of death until two days later when our primary care physician called. James had died from Meningococcal meningitis that had progressed to sepsis.

It was the first time I'd ever heard the word "sepsis."

Unfortunately, it wouldn't be my last.

The First Time: February 2016

The cold started on Christmas Day 2015. I had no idea it would nearly kill me.

Just a cold, I told myself. Nothing serious. By January, it had morphed into bronchitis that wouldn't quit. Then came the abscess—the size of a grapefruit—and I was still trying to treat it at home with natural remedies because they'd worked before.

By the time I got to the emergency room on February 1, 2016, my body was in crisis. They diagnosed me within two hours and admitted me immediately. That evening, I was in surgery.

When the nurses informed me I was septic, terror flooded through me.

Because sepsis—the very illness that had killed my husband seven years earlier—was now trying to take me too.

I completely lost it. I remember sobbing, saying over and over, "This is what killed James. This is what killed James."

Nine days in the hospital. Surgery. A PICC line. Then fifteen days at home connected to an infusion pump that administered high doses of antibiotics 24/7. My kidneys had started to fail and shut down. My blood sugar shot through the roof. My blood count was totally abnormal. The fevers, chills, diarrhea, and depression were relentless.

The pain was the worst I'd ever experienced.

All I can say is: But God.

However, survival came with a cost. My body was never the same. The recovery was long, painful, and left me questioning everything about how I'd been living. For sixteen years as a caregiver, I'd treated my body like a tool—something to be used in service of everyone else.

Sepsis forced me to reckon with the price I'd been paying.

The Second Time: August 2020

We were home in the middle of COVID-19 when it started. An abscess developed. I recognized the warning signs this time—when the fever started and wouldn't break, when the abscess became hot to touch and painful, I knew.

This was particularly heartbreaking because I had just started a wellness tea business in late June 2020 to help people heal from COVID. I was trying to help others heal while my own body was breaking down again.

The irony wasn't lost on me.

Back to the hospital. Back to surgery. Back to the PICC line and infusion pump. Back to the fear that this time, I wouldn't make it.

But the worst was still to come.

During recovery, I noticed my ankle started to swell. Initially, I thought it was a side effect of one of the medications. The swelling in my ankle went down, but then my right great toe became inflamed. I noticed it had an open wound.

This developed into osteomyelitis—a bone infection. The doctor did everything possible to save my toe, but it was too late. We were faced with a difficult decision: aggressive treatment with uncertain outcomes, or amputation to prevent losing my entire right foot.

I chose amputation. I didn't want to wait and possibly lose my foot. The decision was swift, but the emotional weight of it lingered.

I had already lost my husband to sepsis. Now I was losing parts of my own body to it.

The Third Time: October 2020

Just two months after the amputation, sepsis came for me again.

By this point, I felt deflated—like my life was slipping away in pieces. The physical toll was immense. The emotional exhaustion was overwhelming. I remember the sterility of the hospital rooms, the hum of the machines, and the weight of the realization that I was no longer just the woman sitting by the bed—I was the one in it.

Again.

Each time I slipped toward the edge, I felt the pull of what I call "The Great Interruption." The place where life pauses and death whispers. The threshold where you have to decide: Do I keep fighting? Do I choose to stay?

But each time, I was sent back.

Three times. I walked through death's door three times. And three times, I chose life.

Yet something fundamental had shifted by the third time. Survival was no longer enough. I couldn't just choose to survive anymore.

I had to choose to LIVE—fully, intentionally, and no longer in service to everyone but myself.

The Teaching: Survival Is a Mandate

Walking through death's door three times and being returned to the land of the living is not a coincidence. It is a mandate.

You do not survive the unsurvivable just to return to a life of quiet depletion. You aren't spared so you can go back to being a "world-class sacrifice" for everyone else.

If you have survived what should have killed you—whether that was a physical illness, a crushing loss, or a decade of soul-crushing caregiving—your life is no longer your own. It is a Kingdom assignment.

And that assignment requires you to be whole.

When you are fighting for your life, you are forced into a brutal kind of embodiment. You can no longer ignore your heart rate, your breath, or your pain. Death is a master teacher of presence. It strips away the non-essentials and leaves you with a single, burning truth:

You are still here.

But there is a dangerous gap between surviving and choosing yourself.

Survival is reactive. It is the body's instinctive refusal to quit. Choosing yourself, however, is proactive. It is the soul's decision to thrive.

For years after each bout with sepsis, I was a survivor, but I hadn't yet made the choice to live for Karen. I was living for the assignment of caregiving, for the memory of James, and for the needs of my family.

I was still performing survival. I had not yet stepped into sovereignty.

What Death Taught Me About Living

Each time I came back from death's door, I learned something I couldn't have learned any other way. These aren't theoretical lessons. They're truths written in scar tissue, in missing toes, in PICC line marks, and in the terror of hearing "You're septic" for the third time.

Lesson 1: Your Body Is Not Optional

For sixteen years as a caregiver, my body was a tool for serving others. Through sepsis, my body became a battlefield. But survival taught me something crucial: my body is neither a tool nor a battlefield.

It's a temple.

Sepsis forced me to pay attention in ways I'd been avoiding for years. You can't ignore your body when it's shutting down. You can't push through when your organs are failing. You can't treat it as expendable when it's literally fighting for its life.

I had to learn—am still learning—to treat my body with the reverence it deserves. Not as something to be used up, but as something to be stewarded with wisdom and care.

This is what 1 Corinthians 6:19 means in practice: "Do you not know that your bodies are temples of the Holy Spirit, who is in you, whom you have received from God?"

Your body isn't just a vessel for doing. It's the sacred space where you experience being alive.

Lesson 2: Rest Is Not a Luxury—It's Survival

Sepsis doesn't care about your to-do list. It doesn't care about deadlines, obligations, or who needs you. It will force you to rest whether you choose it or not.

During each recovery, I had no choice but to surrender to rest. My body demanded it. There was no hustling my way back to health, no pushing through the exhaustion. My body would shut down completely if I didn't honor its need for stillness.

This is what taught me about true Sabbath rest. Rest isn't something you earn after you've done enough. It's not a reward for productivity. Rest is a requirement for survival. It's how your body heals. It's how your soul restores itself.

I learned that rest is not a luxury reserved for when everything else is done. Rest is the foundation upon which everything else must be built.

Lesson 3: Choosing Life Means Choosing Yourself

Each time I survived sepsis, I faced a choice. Not just "Do I want to live?" but "HOW do I want to live?"

After the first time in 2016, I went back to my old patterns. Caregiving. Pushing. Sacrificing. After the second time in August 2020, I started to question those patterns. By the third time in October 2020, I couldn't go back anymore.

Something had fundamentally shifted.

I realized that choosing life meant choosing to live for myself, not just for everyone else. It meant actively choosing embodiment over dissociation. Choosing sovereignty over servitude. It meant choosing myself as worthy of the same care I'd given to everyone else.

This wasn't selfishness. This was survival. This was finally understanding that I couldn't love others well while abandoning myself completely.

Lesson 4: You Can't Pour From Empty—And Empty Will Kill You
My body broke down because I'd been running on empty for years. Sixteen years of caregiving. Sixteen years of giving everything away. Sixteen years of treating my own needs as optional while everyone else's needs were urgent.

Sepsis was my body's way of screaming: "ENOUGH. You can't keep sacrificing me for everyone else."

This is why I'm so adamant now about teaching women that self-care isn't selfish—it's stewardship. You cannot pour from an empty cup. And if you keep trying, eventually your body will stop you.

Sometimes permanently.

The cost of chronic depletion isn't just exhaustion or burnout. The cost can be your life.

Lesson 5: There Is Life After Death
I'm not the same woman who survived sepsis in 2016. Or August 2020. Or October 2020. Each time I walked through death's door, something of the old Karen stayed behind. And something new emerged.

This is what I mean when I talk about becoming. Not just surviving, but being transformed through the fire. Dying to old patterns. Emerging into new ways of being.

I grieve the woman I was before sepsis. But I also honor what she survived and what she learned. There is life after death—literal and metaphorical. You can be reborn into a fuller version of yourself, even through trauma.

Maybe especially through trauma.

Interrupting the Interruption
Trauma—like three bouts of sepsis—pauses your identity. It freezes you in a state of emergency where all you can think about is survival. To emerge, you have to "interrupt the interruption." You have to decide that the trauma no longer gets to dictate the pace of your life.

Restarting at 57 isn't about reclaiming your youth. It's about reclaiming your sovereignty. It's about realizing that if God kept you here three times, He didn't do it so you could keep playing a supporting role.

He did it so you could become the sanctuary He designed you to be.

The Application: The Choice for Life

Survival has a cost. We often carry the bill in our bodies—in high blood pressure, chronic tension, amputations, scars, and a nervous system that forgot how to feel safe.

But survival also carries wisdom. And that wisdom is what transforms us from victims of our history into architects of our legacy.

Reflection Questions

Take out your journal. These questions aren't rhetorical—they're invitations to honor what you've survived and to choose how you'll live going forward.

1. The Survival Cost
What has "just getting through it" cost your physical and spiritual health?

Where is your body still holding the tension of the years you were in the battlefield? Be specific. Is it in your shoulders? Your jaw? Your stomach? Your sleep patterns?

Write it down. Acknowledge it. This is the first step toward healing.

2. The Wisdom of the Dark
What did your hardest season—your "death door" moment—teach you about what truly matters?

If you could only take three things with you into your new life, what would they be? Not physical things, but truths. Values. Non-negotiables.

For me, it was: My body is a temple. Rest is holy. Choosing myself is sacred stewardship.

What are yours?

3. The Choosing
If survival was God's part of the miracle, what does your part—choosing to thrive—look like today?

What would it mean to honor the fact that you're still here by actually living?

Not just surviving. Not just getting through. But actually building a life that reflects the magnitude of what you've survived.

Meditation: The Mandate

Find a quiet space. Close your eyes. Place your hand on your heart and feel it beating.

That heartbeat is not an accident. You are still here for a reason.

Breathe deeply and repeat these words slowly, letting them sink into your body:

"I survived for a reason. I was spared for a purpose. My life is a Kingdom assignment, and I honor it by choosing to be whole. I am no longer a victim of my history; I am the architect of my legacy."

Say it until you believe it. Say it until your body remembers that it's not just a battlefield—it's a sanctuary.

For Sepsis Survivors

If you're reading this as a sepsis survivor, I see you.

I know the fear doesn't just go away. I know you scan your body constantly for warning signs—every fever, every rapid heartbeat, every moment of confusion sends you spiraling back to those hospital rooms.

I know you're different now. Your body is different. Your relationship to your mortality is different. You're grieving the person you were before, even as you're grateful to be alive.

You're not alone.

Recovery is long. The trauma is real. The fear of recurrence is valid. And becoming whole again is possible—even if you're not the same person you were before.

Maybe especially because you're not.

Resources for Survivors:
- Sepsis Alliance: www.sepsis.org
- Sepsis Alliance Connect (Virtual support community)
- CDC Sepsis Information: www.cdc.gov/sepsis

Warning Signs Everyone Should Know

Sepsis kills more people annually than breast cancer, prostate cancer, and AIDS combined. Every hour of delay in treatment increases mortality risk by 7.6%.

If you or someone you love shows these signs, get to an emergency room immediately:

- High fever or very low body temperature
- Rapid heart rate
- Rapid breathing or shortness of breath
- Confusion or disorientation
- Extreme pain or discomfort
- Clammy or sweaty skin

Time is measured in minutes, not hours.

These were the signs I missed with James. Or more accurately, the signs we didn't understand until it was too late. Don't make the same mistake.

Survival gave me the mandate to live. But surviving sepsis three times while still trapped in Savannah wasn't enough. I had to do something I never thought I'd be capable of: I had to make what I now call the "Sacred Exit." I had to choose myself even when it felt like betrayal. Even when it meant disappointing the people I loved most. In the next chapter, I'll show you what happened when I finally left—and what became possible on the other side.

You are still here. That means something. Honor it by choosing to live—fully, sovereignly, and no longer in depletion.

The cocoon is breaking open. Your mandate is clear. Now it's time to choose yourself.

Chapter 3:
THE SACRED EXIT & THE MOVE TO VEGAS

"Forget the former things; do not dwell on the past.
See, I am doing a new thing! Now it springs up; do you not perceive it?
I am making a way in the wilderness and streams in the wasteland."

~Isaiah 43:18-19

For years, I believed that my presence was the only thing holding the sky up for my family. In Savannah, my identity was inextricably linked to the house, the history, and the heavy, relentless cycle of caregiving. I was the woman who stayed. I was the woman who managed the meds, handled the falls, and carried the grief of a house that had seen too much loss.

I was the anchor. The center. The one who didn't leave.

But on August 27, 2024, the sky fell anyway.

The Day Everything Broke

My mother fell from her wheelchair that morning. It wasn't the first time, but it was the time that changed everything.

As I stood over her, waiting forty-five agonizing minutes for help to arrive, the silence in the room became a mirror. I looked at the floor. I looked at the walls of a life I had built around sacrifice. And I finally saw the truth:

I was drowning in a shallow pool of my own devotion.

When we finally got to the hospital, a social worker pulled me aside. She didn't offer me a brochure on better caregiving techniques. She didn't suggest support groups or respite care options. She looked me directly in the eyes and said words I'd been waiting sixteen years to hear:

"Karen, you need help. You cannot do this anymore."

In that moment, I realized: I had been waiting for someone—anyone—to give me permission to stop. And God, in His mercy, was using a stranger in a hospital hallway to tell me that my assignment as a sacrifice was over.

The decision to place my mother in a skilled nursing facility was the hardest thing I have ever done. It felt like a betrayal of every "strong woman" script I had ever been taught. It felt like failure. It felt like I was abandoning the woman who had raised me, the woman who had moved into my home when she needed me most.

But that evening, I went home and looked in the mirror.

I didn't recognize the woman staring back at me. Her eyes were dull. Her skin was gray with the fatigue of a decade of survival. Her spirit was buried under the needs of others, so deep that even she had forgotten it was there.

I realized then: If I didn't choose myself now, there wouldn't be anything left of me to save.

The Migration: From Savannah to the Mojave

Leaving Savannah wasn't just a move. It was an extraction.

I had to pull myself out of the soil where I was only known for what I could do for others. In that city, I was "the widow." I was "the caregiver." I was "the woman who stayed." Every street corner held a memory of loss. Every room in that house echoed with the footsteps of people who were no longer there.

I couldn't become in the place where I had only learned to survive.

In October 2024, I packed my personal belongings—not the furniture, not the memories, just what was mine—and headed for Denver. My son Benjamin had relocated there years before after his medical retirement from the Air Force. I thought that being near the mountains would be enough. I thought proximity to family would be the answer.

But Denver didn't feel like a destination. It felt like a waiting room.

My soul was still restless. I was no longer a full-time caregiver, but I hadn't yet found my "Sovereign Territory." I was in the in-between—the space after you leave but before you arrive. The messy middle of metamorphosis where the cocoon has cracked but the wings haven't fully formed.

Then came November. Benjamin had relocated to Las Vegas in July, and something in my spirit said: Go.

Crossing the City Limits: November 20, 2024

People think of Vegas as a place of noise and neon, but for me, it represented something entirely different: the vast, open space of the desert.

The desert in the Bible isn't just a place of wandering. It is the place where God takes His people to speak to their hearts. It is where you are stripped of your old roles so you can be clothed in your new authority. Moses met God in the desert. Jesus was tested in the desert. The Israelites wandered forty years in the desert before entering the Promised Land.

The desert is where you die to who you were so you can be reborn into who you're becoming.

I began the drive from Denver to Las Vegas on a Wednesday morning. As I crossed from Colorado into Utah, then from Utah into Nevada, I felt something physical shifting in my chest. The landscape opened up. The sky became impossibly wide. The mountains gave way to mesa and desert floor.

And on November 20th, as I crossed the Las Vegas city limits, I knew.

The moment I saw those mountain silhouettes against the desert sky, something inside me exhaled for the first time since May 5, 2009. For the first time since James transitioned. For the first time since I became "Postponed Karen."

I breathed air that didn't feel heavy with expectation.

I was home. I was finally ready to be found.

The Restoration: A Family Reunited

The move to Vegas wasn't just about my solo journey. It was about the restoration of my family legacy.

In July 2025—eight months after I arrived—my son Benjamin and his wife Nadya relocated to Las Vegas.

As I reflect on this now, I realize that by choosing myself, I actually saved my family. For years, Benjamin and I had lived our lives in parallel. Both of us showing immense courage in different theaters of life, yet separated by thousands of miles. He was medically retired from the Air Force in 2017, building his own life in Denver while I was back in Savannah, surviving sepsis and caregiving.

We talked. We texted. We knew we loved each other. But we weren't *together*. We couldn't just show up at each other's door. We couldn't have Sunday dinners. We couldn't be a family in the daily, ordinary ways that matter most.

When Benjamin told me he and Nadya were moving to Vegas, I cried. Not sad tears—relieved tears. Grateful tears. The kind of tears that come when you realize that by choosing yourself, you actually saved your family.

November 2025 was our first Thanksgiving together since 2011. For fourteen years, we'd celebrated holidays apart—me in Savannah, him wherever the military sent him, and later, in Denver.

But this Thanksgiving, we sat at the same table. In the same city. In our new territory.

And then came Christmas. Our first Christmas together since 2016. Nine years.

Sitting at the table with my son and daughter-in-law in our new city, I realized something profound: By making my "Sacred Exit," I created a space where we could finally be together as *whole people*. Not as a mother-caregiver and a son-soldier. Not as people defined by duty and distance.

But as a family, building our lives in parallel again—this time from a foundation of presence and peace.

Building Your Territory for Influence: The Vegas Advantage

Geography matters for your "becoming." You cannot build a "Sovereign Soft Life" in an environment that is constantly demanding you return to your old, depleted self.

I chose Las Vegas for three reasons:

First, it was where my son was. After years of separation, I could finally be near Benjamin. Family matters. Proximity matters. And for the first time in over a decade, I could build a life where my son was part of my daily reality, not just someone I talked to on the phone.

Second, the desert itself called to me. The openness. The sky. The sense of possibility. In Savannah, everywhere I looked, I saw what I'd lost. In Vegas, everywhere I looked, I saw space for what I could become.

Third, Las Vegas is a city of founders, operators, and high-visibility creatives. It's a city of people managing massive reputations, boutique brands, and the weight of public expectation. These people are successful. They're building empires. But many of them are burning out. They're managing the "noise," but they have no "sanctuary."

What was missing in this territory was wise, grounded, faith-based embodiment coaching. They didn't need more "hustle" advice. They needed someone who had walked through the fire of sepsis and the desert of grief and come out sovereign.

This is my Vegas Advantage. My story of survival makes me the perfect advisor for those who are currently surviving their own success.

By building in public in this new city, I am showing other women that you don't have to stay where you are "needed" if it means losing who you are. You can leave. You can choose yourself. And you can build something beautiful on the other side.

The Teaching: The Theology of the Exit

We often mistake "staying" for "faithfulness." We think that if we leave a hard situation or a demanding role, we are being selfish.

But here's the truth Scripture reveals:

Choosing yourself is not selfish. It is stewardship.

You are a daughter of the King. You are a temple of the Holy Spirit (1 Corinthians 6:19). If you allow your "temple" to be desecrated by constant depletion and boundary-crossing, you are not being a good steward of the life God gave you.

The "Sacred Exit" is the moment you decide that your peace is worth the discomfort of other people's disappointment.

Think about this: Jesus regularly withdrew from the crowds. He left people who still needed healing. He walked away from demands that were legitimate and pressing. Not because He didn't care, but because He knew that to sustain His ministry, He had to protect His communion with the Father.

If Jesus modeled boundaries, why do we think we're supposed to be endlessly available?

The Sacred Exit isn't abandonment. It's alignment. It's recognizing that you cannot pour from empty, and if you keep trying, you won't just burn out—you'll burn up.

To become someone new, you must leave the place where you were only known for your utility.

You must find a "Sovereign Territory" where you can be known for your essence, not just your function. Where people see you as a whole person, not just a role to be filled.

For me, that territory was Las Vegas. For you, it might be a different city. Or it might not be a physical move at all. Your Sacred Exit might be:

- Leaving a career that's consuming you
- Setting a boundary with a family member
- Walking away from a relationship where you've become too small
- Closing a business that's draining your soul
- Saying "no" to an obligation everyone expects you to fulfill

Whatever form it takes, the Sacred Exit requires courage. It requires you to disappoint people. It requires you to trust that God can hold the sky up without you.

And here's what I learned: He can. He always could.

The Application: Mapping Your Sovereign Territory

It is time to define the boundaries of your own emergence. You may not need to move across the country, but you do need to make a "Sacred Exit" from the roles that no longer fit.

1. Reflection: The Cost of Choosing
Take out your journal and answer these questions with radical honesty:

What would your "Sacred Exit" look like?

Is it a physical move? A change in career? A boundary with a family member? A role you need to step back from?

Write it down. Be specific. Don't censor yourself.

What is the one thing you are most afraid will happen if you choose yourself?

Will people be disappointed? Will they think you're selfish? Will they be angry? Write out your worst-case scenario.

Now, ask yourself a harder question:

What will happen to ME if I don't?

If you stay in this role for another year, another five years, another decade—what will it cost your body? Your peace? Your spirit? Your legacy?

Be specific. Because the cost of staying is often higher than the cost of leaving.

2. Mapping Your Territory
Identify your "Vegas"—the place or state of mind where your unique lived experience becomes an advantage rather than a burden.

Who are the people in your sphere who are starving for the wisdom you gained in your "survival" years?

Where do they gather? What do they need that only someone with *your* story can provide?

For me, it's founders and creatives in Vegas who are managing burnout and reputation. For you, it might be different. But there IS a territory where your becoming becomes your advantage.

What "territory" is God calling you to occupy with your new, sovereign voice?

Not the territory where you're needed. The territory where you're *meant to be*.

3. Visualization: Meeting Her
Close your eyes. Take a deep breath.

Imagine yourself six months from now, standing in your new territory. You've made your Sacred Exit. You are rested. You are embodied. You are living a life that doesn't require you to sacrifice your soul to be significant.

How does she stand?

Is her posture different? Is her breathing deeper? Does she take up more space?

How does she speak?

Is her voice clearer? Firmer? Does she say "no" without apologizing?

What is the first thing she says to the "you" of today?

Listen. She has wisdom for you. She knows something you're still learning.

Write down what she says. This is your becoming speaking to your present. Honor it.

You don't have to stay where you're needed at the cost of who you're becoming.

The Sacred Exit isn't abandonment. It's obedience to the call of your own wholeness.

Making the Sacred Exit was the hardest decision of my life. But once I crossed into my sovereign territory, I realized something profound: choosing life wasn't enough. I had to learn how to live IN the body I'd been given back. Three times, God spared my life. But I'd spent fifty-seven years treating my body as a tool, a battlefield, a sacrifice for others.

Now I had to learn what I'd never known: how to inhabit my body as a sanctuary.

That's what Part II is about. Not just surviving. Not just choosing yourself. But learning to live fully present, fully embodied, fully sovereign in the temple God gave you. Because embodiment isn't just a concept—it's the daily practice of becoming the woman you were always meant to be.

The cocoon is breaking open. Your territory is waiting. And you—fully embodied, fully sovereign—are ready to claim it.

Pause Here: A Moment to breathe

You've just walked through three chapters of survival, death, and sacred choice. That's not light reading. That's your life—or a mirror of it.

If you need to stop here and let this settle into your body before continuing, do that.

Embodiment isn't linear. Becoming isn't a race.

This book will still be here when you're ready to continue. Honor your own pace.

Take a walk. Journal. Breathe. Come back when you're ready.

The cocoon is breaking open. But emergence happens in stages, not all at once.

PART II:
KINGDOM EMBODIMENT
(The Temple)

For sixteen years, my body was a tool for serving others. Through three bouts of sepsis, my body was a battlefield. But now, at 57, standing in my Las Vegas sanctuary with my son just minutes away and the desert sky stretched wide above me, I'm learning something I've never known:

What it means to inhabit my body as a temple.

Not just survive in it. Not just push it to perform. But to be fully present, fully alive, fully embodied in the sanctuary God designed me to be.

This is the work of Part II: learning to treat your body with the reverence it deserves, understanding what true strength looks like (the Proverbs 31 woman wasn't exhausted—she was embodied), and discovering your unique expression of protective, sovereign leadership.

Embodiment isn't a destination. It's a daily practice of inhabiting your becoming.

And it starts with the most fundamental truth Scripture offers us:

"Do you not know that your bodies are temples of the Holy Spirit, who is in you, whom you have received from God?" (1 Corinthians 6:19)

The cocoon has broken open. Now it's time to learn what it means to fly.

Chapter 4:
YOUR BODY AS SANCTUARY, NOT SACRIFICE

Do you not know that your bodies are temples of the Holy Spirit, who is in you, whom you have received from God? You are not your own; you were bought at a price. Therefore honor God with your bodies."

~1 Corinthians 6:19-20

The Story: Reclaiming the Temple in the Desert

The first morning in my Las Vegas sanctuary, I was greeted by a silence that felt heavy, almost physical. For sixteen years, my mornings had been dictated by the needs of others—the sound of a walker on hardwood floors at 3 AM, the timing of medications that couldn't be missed, the constant low-grade hum of vigilance that comes with caregiving. My body had become so attuned to the rhythm of someone else's survival that I had forgotten what it felt like to wake up to my own.

But that November morning in 2024, the only sound was my own breath.

I sat on the edge of the bed and did something I hadn't done intentionally in years: I felt my own body. Not as a checklist of things to manage—blood pressure, pain levels, how much sleep I didn't get—but as a presence. As something that deserved my attention not because it was breaking down, but simply because it was mine.

For nearly two decades, I had treated my physical frame as a tool for endurance. I used it to carry the weight of grief after losing James in 2009. I used it to lift my mother when she fell, to stand between my family and collapse, to keep moving when everything in me wanted to stop. I used it until it broke. Three times.

I looked down at my right foot. The space where my great toe used to be was a stark reminder of the price I'd paid for treating my body as expendable. For years, I had viewed my scars—the faint lines from PICC insertions on my arms, the surgical marks from three bouts with sepsis, the amputation itself—as evidence of failure. I felt like a "cut back" version of the woman I used to be. Diminished. Less than whole.

But in the quiet of that desert morning, something shifted.

The Holy Spirit began to reframe my scars.

My body hadn't failed me. It had been loyal to me. Through what I call "The Great Interruption"—those three times I walked through death's door—my body had fought for me. It had refused to quit even when I was asking too much of it. It had survived sepsis not once, not twice, but three times. Most people don't survive once.

I realized then that I had spent sixteen years being a "world-class sacrifice" for everyone else's survival, but I had never been a sanctuary for my own soul. I was "Postponed Karen," living on permanent mute, treating my body like a warehouse for everyone else's needs while ignoring the temple God had given me.

That day in the desert, I had to learn a new kind of walk.

Literally, my center of gravity had shifted after the amputation. I had to relearn balance, relearn how my weight distributed, relearn what felt stable. But the physical adjustment was nothing compared to the spiritual one.

*My center of gravity had to move from **utility** (what I could do for others) to **presence** (how I showed up for God and for myself).*

I was no longer in the emergency room. The season of survival was over. The season of becoming had begun.

And becoming required me to finally inhabit the body I'd been given—not as a tool to be used up, but as a temple to be honored.

The Teaching: From Tool to Temple

The Lie We Believe
We often frame our self-neglect as a spiritual virtue. We tell ourselves that being "poured out" is the ultimate sign of a Kingdom woman. We quote Philippians 2:17 about being "poured out like a drink offering" and use it to justify exhaustion, depletion, and the slow erosion of our own well-being.

But we must distinguish between being **poured out** and being **hollowed out**.

One is an act of overflow; the other is an act of depletion.

For sixteen years, I lived in the hollow. I believed the lie that to be holy was to be erased. That my value was measured by how much I could disappear for the sake of others. That the most spiritual thing I could do was treat my body as a tool—something functional, expendable, meant to be used until it wore out.

But that's not what Scripture teaches.

The Body as Temple: What It Really Means
In 1 Corinthians 6:19, Paul writes: "Do you not know that your bodies are temples of the Holy Spirit, who is in you, whom you have received from God? You are not your own."

For years, I only heard the second part: "You are not your own." I interpreted that as permission to give myself away completely. But I missed the first part—the part that changes everything:

Your body is a temple.

Not a warehouse. Not a tool shed. Not a sacrifice on someone else's altar.

A temple.

*A temple is a place of **presence**. It's where God dwells. It's sacred space that must be honored, protected, stewarded with reverence. You don't treat a temple like you treat a warehouse. You don't pile junk in the corners and ignore the structure until it collapses.*

When you understand your body as temple, everything changes:

- ***Utility becomes secondary to presence.*** *You stop asking "How much can I do?" and start asking "How fully can I be present?"*

- ***Function becomes secondary to stewardship.*** *You stop treating your body like something to use up and start treating it like something to honor.*

- ***Performance becomes secondary to wholeness.*** *You stop measuring your worth by your output and start recognizing your inherent value as God's dwelling place.*

This is Kingdom Embodiment: the shift from **Tool to Temple**, *from* **Utility to Sanctuary**, *from* **Sacrifice to Stewardship**.

Survival Forces Embodiment

When you're fighting for your life, you can no longer ignore your body.

During my three battles with sepsis, I was forced into a brutal kind of embodiment. I couldn't push through when my organs were failing. I couldn't ignore my heart rate, my breath, my pain. I couldn't treat my body as optional when it was literally the only thing standing between me and death.

Death is a master teacher of presence. It strips away everything non-essential and leaves you with one burning truth:

You are still here.

And if you're still here, your body—scarred, tired, imperfect as it is—deserves your reverence.

*You do not survive what should have killed you just to return to a life of quiet depletion. If you have been spared—whether from illness, loss, or a decade of soul-crushing caregiving—your life is a Kingdom assignment. And that assignment requires you to be **whole**, not just functional.*

Stewardship Over Sacrifice

There's a profound difference between stewardship and sacrifice.

***Sacrifice** says: "I give up my body, my health, my rest for the sake of others. This is what love requires."*

***Stewardship** says: "I honor the body God gave me, knowing that I cannot love others well if I am hollowed out. This is what wisdom requires."*

Choosing yourself isn't abandonment. It's the ultimate act of stewardship.

You cannot teach others to honor their bodies as temples if you're still treating yours like an expendable tool. You cannot pour from empty. And if you keep trying, eventually your body will stop you—sometimes permanently.

This is what happened to me. Sepsis was my body's way of screaming: "ENOUGH. You can't keep sacrificing me for everyone else."

The Shift: From Reactive to Proactive

Survival is reactive. It's your body's instinctive refusal to quit even when you've asked too much of it.

*But **choosing to thrive** is proactive. It's your soul's decision to finally honor the temple you've been given.*

*For years after each bout with sepsis, I was a survivor, but I hadn't yet made the choice to live **for Karen**. I was still living for the assignment of caregiving, for the memory of James, for the needs of everyone around me.*

I was still performing survival. I had not yet stepped into sovereignty.

The shift happens when you realize: **The emergency is over. I am no longer in the ICU. The season of becoming has begun.**

And becoming requires you to move from:
- **Endurance to Embodiment**
- **Function to Presence**
- **Tool to Temple**

This is not selfishness. This is sacred work.

The Application: The Embodiment Audit

Leaving the "survival cocoon" requires an honest look at how you currently inhabit your body. You cannot heal what you refuse to acknowledge.

Before we can build a life of embodied sovereignty, we must first honor where we've been and what we've been carrying.

THE APPLICATION: Choose Your Entry Point

You don't have to do all of these exercises right now. Choose the one that feels most urgent for where you are today. You can always come back to the others.

If you're struggling to feel safe in your body: *Start with* **Locate the "Survival Noise"**

If you're carrying weight that isn't yours: *Start with* **The 15% Weight Release**

If you're disconnected from your body: *Start with* **The Gratitude Scan**

If you're ready to commit to this work: *Start with* **The Temple Vow**

If you want to build a daily practice: *Start with* **The Embodied Morning Practice**

1. Locate the "Survival Noise"

Your body stores the stress of being "the strong one." For years, you've been operating in survival mode, and your nervous system hasn't gotten the message that the emergency is over.

Where does your body hold the tension?

Stop right now. Close your eyes. Take three slow breaths.

Now scan your body from head to toe:
- *Is your jaw clenched?*
- *Are your shoulders up by your ears?*
- *Is there tightness in your chest?*
- *Pain in your lower back?*
- *Tension in your stomach?*

This is where you've been storing the weight of holding the center for everyone else.

The Practice:

Three times today, stop what you're doing. Place your hand on the area where you hold the most tension. Breathe into that space. And say out loud:

"You are safe. We are no longer in the emergency room. The season of survival is over."

Your body needs to hear this. Your nervous system needs permission to stand down from high alert.

2. The 15% Weight Release

You're pre-ordering this book at a 15% discount because I want to reward your early commitment to your own becoming. Now I want you to apply that same "15%" to your physical and emotional load.

You are carrying weight that isn't yours to hold.

Identify one task, one obligation, or one burden you are carrying that is not yours.

It might be:

- *A responsibility someone else needs to step up and handle*
- *An expectation you've been trying to meet that isn't aligned with your season*
- *A role you've been performing out of guilt rather than calling*
- *Physical clutter in your home that you're keeping "just in case"*
- *Emotional labor you're doing for someone who needs to do it for themselves*

This week, release 15% of your load.

Not everything. Just 15%. One thing.

Think of it as a "15% discount" on your stress levels. A down payment on your sovereign soft life.

3. The Gratitude Scan: Honoring Your Body's Loyalty

This exercise doesn't require a mirror. It only requires presence.

Find a quiet space. Sit comfortably or lie down. Close your eyes.

We're going to do a body scan—not to judge or fix anything, but simply to acknowledge and thank the body that's been carrying you.

Start with your heart.

Place your hand on your chest. Feel it beating.

Say out loud or silently: "Thank you, heart, for beating through the hardest days. For refusing to quit even when I wanted to. For keeping me alive."

Move to your lungs.

Take a deep breath. Feel your lungs expand.

Say: "Thank you, lungs, for breathing when I forgot how. For filling me with life even in the darkest moments."

Move to your stomach.

Place your hand on your belly.

Say: "Thank you, stomach, for processing the stress, the fear, the grief. For holding what I couldn't speak."

Move to your legs.

Place your hands on your thighs.

Say: "Thank you, legs, for carrying me when I thought I couldn't go on. For standing when I wanted to collapse."

Move to your hands.

Look at your hands. Open and close them.

Say: "Thank you, hands, for serving, for holding, for caring. For doing the work even when I was exhausted."

Finally, place both hands on your heart again.

Say: "Thank you, body, for being loyal to me even when I abandoned you. I see you now. I honor you. And I'm learning to treat you as the temple you are."

Sit in this for as long as you need.

This is embodiment: presence without judgment. Gratitude without performance.

Write a one-sentence "Honor Statement" for your body:

Here's mine:

"Thank you for being loyal to me even when I was hollowing you out. Thank you for fighting for me three times when I should have died. Today, I choose to be a sanctuary."

Now write yours.

4. The Temple Vow
If your body is a temple, you are its steward. And stewards take vows.

Place your hand on your heart. Say this out loud:

"I vow to treat my body as the temple it is. I will no longer sacrifice it for the convenience of others. I will steward it with wisdom, honor it with rest, and inhabit it with presence. I am no longer a tool. I am a sanctuary. And I will live like it."

This isn't a one-time declaration. This is a daily practice of choosing embodiment over dissociation, presence over performance, sanctuary over sacrifice.

5. The Embodied Morning Practice
For the next seven days, practice this simple morning ritual:

Before you check your phone. Before you think about your to-do list. Before you respond to anyone else's needs:

1. **Sit on the edge of your bed**
2. **Place both feet flat on the floor**
3. **Feel the weight of your body**
4. **Take five slow breaths**
5. **Say out loud:** *"I am present. I am embodied. My body is a temple, and today I will honor it."*

This simple practice rewires your nervous system. It teaches your body that you are no longer in emergency mode. It reminds you that presence—not productivity—is your first priority.

The Truth About Your Body

Your body has been loyal to you.

Even when you ignored it. Even when you pushed it past its limits. Even when you treated it like a tool instead of a temple.

It kept showing up. It kept fighting. It kept you alive.

Now it's time for you to be loyal to it.

Not someday. Not when everything else is handled. Not when you've finally "earned" the right to rest.

Now.

Because you are no longer in the cocoon of survival. You are in the season of becoming. And becoming requires you to finally—fully—inhabit the sanctuary God gave you.

Your body is not a warehouse for other people's needs.

Your body is not a tool to be used until it breaks.

Your body is not a sacrifice on someone else's altar.

Your body is a temple. And it's time to treat it like one.

In the next chapter, we'll explore what it means to protect that temple—not through combat, but through the sovereign strength of a woman who knows her worth and guards her peace. Because once you understand that your body is a sanctuary, the next step is learning to be its warrior.

The cocoon is breaking open. Your embodiment has begun. And the woman you're becoming? She knows she's a temple, not a tool.

You are not too late. You are exactly on time.

REMEMBER THIS

- My body is a temple (1 Corinthians 6:19), not a warehouse for everyone else's needs.
- Survival forced me into embodiment—now I choose it daily.
- Stewardship of self IS Kingdom work.
- I cannot pour from empty—and empty will kill me.
- Choosing myself isn't abandonment; it's alignment.
- I am no longer a tool. I am a sanctuary.

Chapter 5:
THE WARRIOR ARCHETYPE & PROTECTIVE LEADERSHIP

"She is clothed with strength and dignity; she can laugh at the days to come."

~ Proverbs 31:25

The Story: The Mirror in the Warrior Women

I remember the moment I first saw the *Dora Milaje* on screen in *Black Panther*. Those warrior women—fierce, disciplined, moving with a grace that somehow contained both softness and steel—struck something deep in my soul.

I couldn't explain it then. I just knew I was transfixed.

Later, when I watched *The Woman King* and learned about the real *Dahomey Amazons* who inspired the film, that same recognition washed over me. These weren't just entertaining movie characters. They were mirrors reflecting something I had always carried but never had language for.

For months, I kept coming back to these images. I'd scroll through photos of the Dahomey warriors—women who protected their kingdom, who trained their bodies as instruments of both beauty and battle, who moved through the world with an unapologetic presence that demanded respect.

I started to wonder why I was so drawn to this archetype. Was it just aesthetic preference? Was it escapism—wishing I could be fierce and powerful instead of tired and depleted?

But the more I sat with it, the more I realized: These women weren't random preferences. They were mirrors.

They reflected something I had been doing all along, but in a form I'd never recognized as strength.

For sixteen years, I had been a warrior. But I'd been fighting the wrong battles—not the battle to care for my mother (that was sacred), but the battle against my own body, my own rest, my own worthiness. I was at war with myself instead of protecting what mattered most: my wholeness.

I had been in combat with exhaustion, trying to prove I could carry more. I had been at war with my own body, pushing it past its breaking point three times. I had been battling guilt every time I even thought about choosing myself.

I was wearing warrior energy—but I was using it to hollow myself out, not to protect what mattered.

The Dahomey Amazons didn't fight because they were perpetually at war. They fought to protect their kingdom, their people, their way of life. They maintained the perimeter so peace could exist inside it.

They didn't fight to prove they were strong. They fought because they were strong—and they knew what they were protecting was worth defending.

That's when I understood what I was really responding to in these warrior women:

Protection as a way of being.

Not combat. Not constant battle. Not hardness for the sake of hardness.

But the sovereign strength of a woman who knows what she's protecting—and refuses to let anything violate it.

The Teaching: Protective Leadership & The Perimeter of Peace

What Protective Leadership Actually Means
When I first started talking about "protective leadership," people would sometimes ask if I was pivoting into executive protection or security work.

But that's not what this is about.

Protective Leadership is the recognition that as a sovereign woman, you are the guardian of your own temple. You are the keeper of your peace, the steward of your boundaries, the protector of your legacy.

You don't need a title or a uniform to be a protector. You need clarity about what you're protecting—and the strength to maintain the perimeter around it.

Think about the Proverbs 31 woman. She wasn't just a business builder and a household manager. She was also wise enough to protect what she built.

"She watches over the affairs of her household" (Proverbs 31:27). That word "watches over"—it's not passive. It's active guardianship. She's alert. She's discerning. She doesn't let chaos, depletion, or misalignment cross her threshold.

This is Protective Leadership: You guard what God gave you to steward.

You protect your body (the temple). You protect your peace (the Sabbath). You protect your calling (the Kingdom assignment). You protect your legacy (the impact that outlives you).

And you do it not through constant combat, but through embodied sovereignty—the quiet, steady strength of a woman who knows her worth and won't apologize for protecting it.

The Warrior Energy Maintains the Soft Life
Here's what most people misunderstand about the "Sovereign Soft Life": It's not possible without warrior energy.

Softness without a perimeter is just vulnerability. It's why so many women who try to rest end up exhausted anyway—because they never set the boundaries that would allow rest to actually happen.

The Dahomey Amazons weren't at war 24/7. They trained. They protected. And when there was no immediate threat, they lived. They had families. They had rituals. They had lives beyond combat.

But when a threat came to their kingdom's borders, they were ready. Because they had maintained their strength specifically so peace could exist inside the perimeter.

This is how warrior energy serves the soft life:
- **You use discipline to protect your rest** (saying no to Sunday work so you can honor Sabbath)

- **You use discernment to protect your peace** (not every opportunity is yours to take)

- **You use boundaries to protect your energy** (not everyone deserves access to your temple)

- **You use your story to protect other women** (showing them they're not alone in their survival)

The warrior doesn't fight for the sake of fighting. She fights—or more accurately, she guards—so that the sacred can flourish.

Strength Without Apology

For too long, we've been taught that our strength is a problem that needs to be softened, explained, or justified.

We apologize for our boundaries. We downplay our capabilities. We make ourselves smaller so others feel comfortable.

But the Dora Milaje don't apologize for their strength. The Dahomey warriors didn't shrink themselves. The Proverbs 31 woman didn't ask permission to be "clothed with strength and dignity."

Strength without apology means:
- You don't explain why you need rest
- You don't justify why you said no
- You don't apologize for protecting your peace
- You don't shrink your presence to make others comfortable
- You don't perform weakness to seem more "feminine" or "accessible"

This isn't arrogance. This is alignment.

When your body, mind, and spirit are aligned with protection, honor, and legacy, you stop performing and start being. You don't have to prove you're strong because your strength is simply part of who you are—and you use it intentionally, not reactively.

Why Strength Doesn't Have to Be "Hard"

I used to think being a warrior meant being hard. Unyielding. Impenetrable.

But the more I studied these warrior women—and the more I stepped into my own protective leadership—I realized: Strength and hardness are not the same thing.

Hardness is what happens when you're in perpetual combat. When you can't let your guard down because you never feel safe. When you've been hurt so many times that you build walls instead of boundaries.

But strength is what happens when you're sovereign. When you know who you are, what you're protecting, and where your perimeter is.

The Dahomey warriors were disciplined, yes. Fierce, absolutely. But they also danced. They sang. They had rituals of joy and connection. Because their strength wasn't about being hard—it was about being whole.

You can be strong and soft. Protective and gentle. Sovereign and tender.

In fact, true softness is only possible when you're strong enough to maintain the boundaries that protect it.

This is what I'm learning in my Vegas sanctuary: I don't need to be hard to be safe. I need to be clear. Clear about what's mine to protect. Clear about where my perimeter is. Clear about who gets access to my temple.

And that clarity—that embodied sovereignty—is what allows me to finally be soft.

How You Protect: The Four Dimensions of Protective Leadership

As I've stepped into this work, I've realized that my warrior energy now serves a different purpose than it did during the sixteen years of survival. I'm no longer fighting for my own life. I'm protecting the becoming of the women I serve.

Here's how protective leadership shows up in my work—and how it can show up in yours:

1. You Protect Through Your Advisory Work
When I work with women as an advisor, I'm not just helping them "do more" or "grow faster." I'm helping them protect what matters.

I protect their peace by teaching them to build Sabbath-honoring businesses that don't consume them.

I protect their boundaries by showing them how to say no without guilt, how to design a life with intentional perimeters.

I protect their reputation by helping them move with the precision and discernment of the P.R.I.V.É. framework—no random decisions, no reactive chaos.

I protect their legacy by helping them build from overflow, not depletion, so they have something sustainable to pass on.

2. You Protect Through Your Wisdom
Every hard lesson I learned in the survival years—every bout with sepsis, every moment of choosing to stop before my body forced me to—is now protective wisdom for other women.

I protect women from the burnout I almost died from by teaching them that rest is not optional.

I protect them from misalignment by showing them how to distinguish between what God called them to and what guilt is pressuring them to do.

I protect them from self-abandonment by modeling what it looks like to choose yourself and still be a woman of faith.

My scars are their shields. My story is their permission slip.

3. You Protect Through Your Story
When I share my journey—the three deaths, the Sacred Exit, the move to Vegas, the choice to prioritize my own becoming—I'm not just being vulnerable. I'm protecting other women from shame.

I'm protecting them from the isolation of thinking they're the only one who's tired.

I'm protecting them from the guilt of thinking that choosing themselves means abandoning their faith.

I'm protecting them from giving up because they think it's "too late" at 47, 52, 57, 63.

Your story, when shared with intention, becomes a perimeter of permission around other women. It says: "If she can choose herself, maybe I can too."

4. You Protect Through Your Presence
There's a reason my Vegas sanctuary feels like sacred space. There's a reason women feel safe in my presence—whether in person, on a call, or through my writing.

It's because I've learned to be a Safe Harbor.

I've survived the storms they're currently in. I know what it's like to walk through death's door. I know what it's like to choose yourself when it feels like betrayal. I know what it's like to rebuild at 57.

My presence—my embodied sovereignty—creates a protected space where transformation can happen. Because they know I'm not going to judge them, push them, or ask them to sacrifice themselves again.

I'm going to help them protect what God gave them to steward.

The Application: Guarding Your Sanctuary

Protective leadership begins with an honest audit of what's currently crossing your perimeter—and what needs to be kept out.

THE APPLICATION: Choose Your Entry Point

You don't have to do all of these exercises right now. Choose the one that calls to you today.

If you need to set a boundary this week: Start with **The Perimeter Check**

If you're unclear about what you're protecting: Start with **Reflection: What Are You Protecting?**

If you're ready to claim your warrior energy: Start with **The Warrior Persona Exercise**

If you want to build a daily practice: Start with **The Daily Practice: Morning Perimeter Check**

1. The Perimeter Check

Your sanctuary—your body, your home, your schedule, your peace—is only as secure as its perimeter.

Take out your journal and answer these questions:

What are you currently allowing into your sanctuary that violates your peace?

Be specific:

- Is it a relationship that consistently depletes you?
- Is it a client who doesn't respect your boundaries?
- Is it a habit of checking email on Sabbath?
- Is it your own inner critic telling you you're selfish for resting?
- Is it a family obligation you've been carrying out of guilt, not calling?

What one thing will you remove from your perimeter this week?

Not everything. Just one thing. Think of it as the first guard you're posting at your gate.

Maybe it's:

- Blocking someone on social media who triggers your old patterns
- Ending a business relationship that's consuming more than it's serving
- Deleting an app that steals your peace
- Having a conversation that sets a new boundary
- Stopping a habit that no longer serves your becoming

Write it down. Make it specific. Do it this week.

2. Reflection: What Are You Protecting?
Protective leadership requires clarity about what you're actually guarding.

Answer these questions:

What are you protecting?

Your health? Your relationship with your son? Your Sabbath? Your creative energy? Your calling? Your legacy? Your peace?

Name it specifically. Write it down.

What needs your protective leadership right now?

Where have you been too "soft" in your boundaries (letting things in that shouldn't be there)?

Where have you been too "hard" on yourself (being your own harshest critic instead of your own protector)?

If you were the warrior at the gate of your own life, what would you refuse to let through?

Chaos? Depletion? Guilt? Self-abandonment? Other people's emergencies that aren't yours to solve?

3. The Warrior Persona Exercise
If you were to name the Warrior Archetype within you—the version of you that survived sepsis, chose the Sacred Exit, and is now building in the desert—what would she look like?

Close your eyes. Imagine her standing at the gate of your sanctuary.

How does she stand? Shoulders back? Feet planted? Eyes clear?

How does she speak when someone tries to guilt-trip you into violating your own boundaries?

What does she say when the old patterns try to creep back in?

How does she protect your peace without apology?

Write a "Decree of Protection" for your life:

Here's mine:

"I, Karen Y. Moore, am the Sovereign Leader of this life. I protect my peace with the same strength I used to survive death three times. My sanctuary is closed to all that depletes my Kingdom assignment. I guard my Sabbath. I steward my temple. I maintain the perimeter so the soft life can flourish. I am both warrior and sanctuary. And I will not apologize for protecting what God gave me to steward."

Now write yours.

Say it out loud. Let your body hear it. Let your nervous system know: You are protected now. The warrior is awake.

4. The Daily Practice: Morning Perimeter Check

For the next seven days, add this to your morning embodiment practice:

After you've placed your feet on the floor and taken your five breaths, ask yourself:

"What am I protecting today? What will I not allow past my perimeter?"

Then set one intentional boundary for that day.

Maybe it's:

- "I will not check work email before 9 AM."
- "I will not apologize for leaving the family gathering early."
- "I will not engage with that person who always tries to guilt me."
- "I will not work through lunch."

One boundary. One day. One act of protective leadership.

Over time, these daily acts build a fortress of sovereignty around your becoming.

The Truth About Warrior Energy

You are not a warrior because you're in constant combat.

You're a warrior because you know what you're protecting—and you refuse to let anything violate it.

Your warrior energy doesn't make you hard. It makes you sovereign. It gives you the strength to maintain the boundaries that allow softness to exist.

You are the Dora Milaje of your own life. The Dahomey Amazon of your own kingdom. The guardian of your own temple.

And the only battle you're fighting now is the one that keeps the perimeter secure so the Sovereign Soft Life can flourish inside it.

You don't need to apologize for your strength. You don't need to shrink your presence. You don't need to perform weakness to be loved.

You need to be embodied. Aligned. Clear.

You need to know what you're protecting and stand at the gate with quiet, unshakeable sovereignty.

This is not about being a bodyguard. This is about being the steward of your own sacred space.

And that, sister, is the work of a warrior.

In the next chapter, we'll explore the woman who perfectly embodies this balance of strength and softness, of discipline and rest, of protection and provision: The Proverbs 31 Woman—not as the exhausted martyr culture made her out to be, but as the sovereign, embodied leader she actually was.

You are emerging. The warrior is awake. And the woman you're becoming? She knows exactly what she's protecting.

You are not too late. You are exactly on time.

Chapter 6:
THE PROVERBS 31 WOMAN REIMAGINED

"She sets about her work vigorously; her arms are strong for her tasks... She speaks with wisdom, and faithful instruction is on her tongue."

~Proverbs 31:17, 26

The Story: Rejecting the Martyr for the Architect

For years, I looked at the woman described in Proverbs 31 with a mixture of exhaustion and resentment.

In the circles I ran in—and perhaps in yours—she was held up as the ultimate standard for the Kingdom woman: a tireless, selfless, sleep-deprived marathon runner who did it all, for everyone, all the time.

I saw her as the original "Postponed Woman." I imagined her up before dawn, sewing by candlelight, managing servants, and running a vineyard, all while making sure her husband's reputation was spotless at the city gates. I assumed she was as tired as I was. I assumed she, too, wore her depletion like a badge of holiness.

And honestly? That version of her made me angry.

Because if *she* was the standard—the woman who never stopped, who never rested, who gave everything away until there was nothing left—then what hope did I have? I was already depleted from sixteen years of caregiving. I'd already survived sepsis three times. I'd already lost parts of my body to the belief that sacrifice was the highest form of love.

If the Proverbs 31 woman was just another exhausted martyr, then I was failing. And I didn't have the energy to fail any harder.

But then I turned 57. I survived sepsis for the third time. I made my "Sacred Exit" from Savannah and arrived in the quiet of my Las Vegas sanctuary. And in that stillness, I picked up the Word and looked at her again—not through the lens of survival, but through the lens of sovereignty.

I realized I had been sold a trope.

Culture—even church culture—had turned a Chief Legacy Architect into an Exhausted Housewife. We had framed her strength as a sacrifice of her body, when the text actually says her strength was her *clothing*. We had read "She gets up while it is still night" (31:15) as proof that she was sleep-deprived and exhausted, when it actually means she was *prepared*. She rose early not because she was in crisis mode, but because she had built a life with such clear boundaries and rhythm that she could afford to.

The woman in Proverbs 31 wasn't a martyr. She was embodied.

She wasn't hollowed out; she was building from overflow.

She wasn't performing strength to keep everyone happy; she was strong because she stewarded her own life first.

I decided then that I was done with the "martyred housewife" version of her. I didn't want to be "Making-it-work Karen" anymore. I wanted to be the woman who laughs at the future because she has built a perimeter around her peace.

I wanted to be *her*—not the cultural caricature, but the woman Scripture actually describes.

The Teaching: The Sovereign Soft Life Model

The Proverbs 31 woman is the ultimate blueprint for the Sovereign Soft Life. When you strip away the modern pressure to "hustle harder," you see a woman whose life is a masterclass in Kingdom embodiment.

Let's look at who she actually was—not who we've been told she was.

She Was Strong (Proverbs 31:17)

"She sets about her work vigorously; her arms are strong."

This isn't the strength of a woman pushing through a fever to finish the laundry. This isn't the strength of someone running on fumes and caffeine. This is the strength of a woman who treats her body as a sanctuary.

Her arms are strong because she has honored her temple, not because she has used it as an expendable tool.

She didn't get strong by accident. She didn't wake up one day and discover she had arms that could handle the work. She set about her work vigorously—meaning she moved with intention, with purpose, with the kind of energy that only comes from rest and proper stewardship.

This is embodied strength. This is the strength that comes from building your life on a foundation of Sabbath, boundaries, and reverence for the body God gave you.

She Was a Business Builder

She didn't just "have a hobby." She was a strategic entrepreneur.

- She considered a field and bought it (31:16) — She wasn't reactive. She was discerning. She evaluated opportunities and made wise decisions.
- She planted a vineyard (31:16) — She built for legacy, not just survival. Vineyards take years to produce fruit. She was thinking generationally.

- She saw that her trading was profitable (31:18) — She understood numbers. She understood business. She knew how to build wealth.

- She made linen garments and sold them (31:24) — She had multiple revenue streams. She wasn't dependent on a single source of income.

This woman was a Kingdom entrepreneur. She understood that business, when done with wisdom and integrity, is an act of stewardship.

But here's what's crucial: Her business served her life. It didn't consume it.

She wasn't hustling 24/7. She wasn't sacrificing her Sabbath to close one more deal. She wasn't running herself into the ground to prove her worth. She built a business that aligned with her values, honored her boundaries, and created the sovereign soft life.

She Was a Provider from Overflow, Not Depletion

"She opens her arms to the poor and extends her hands to the needy." (31:20)

Notice this: She didn't pour from empty. She didn't give away what she didn't have. She extended her hands because her hands were full.

She was able to be generous because she had first been a good steward of her own household. She provided for her family (31:21). She clothed herself in fine linen and purple (31:22). She built a foundation of wholeness first—and *then* she gave from the overflow.

This is the opposite of what we've been taught as Kingdom women. We've been told that to be holy is to be hollowed out. That to be Christ-like is to give until there's nothing left.

But that's not what Scripture teaches. And it's not what the Proverbs 31 woman modeled.

She was a sanctuary for her household because she was first a sanctuary for herself.

She Was Clothed in Strength and Dignity (31:25)

"She is clothed with strength and dignity; she can laugh at the days to come."

She didn't *wear* exhaustion. She didn't *wear* anxiety or fear or the weight of everyone else's expectations.

She wore strength and dignity.

Dignity is what happens when you stop performing for approval and start living from authority. Dignity is what happens when you know who you are, whose you are, and what you're protecting—and you refuse to apologize for it.

Strength and dignity aren't things you earn by sacrificing yourself. They're what you wear when you've built a life that honors the temple God gave you.

This is embodied sovereignty. This is the woman who knows she's not a tool to be used up, but a sanctuary to be stewarded.

She Was Free from Fear (31:25)

"She can laugh at the days to come."

Let that sink in. She laughed at the future.

Not because she was naive. Not because she didn't face challenges. Not because her life was easy.

She laughed because she was prepared.

She had built what I call a "Sacred Architecture" for her life—a structure that included rest, boundaries, protection, and provision. She had removed unnecessary weight. She had honored Sabbath. She had created multiple streams of income. She had trained her body to be strong.

She wasn't afraid of the future because she had done the work in the present.

This is what the Sovereign Soft Life looks like: a life so well-stewarded, so well-protected, so grounded in Kingdom principles that you can face uncertainty with peace instead of panic.

She Was Wise (31:26)

"She speaks with wisdom, and faithful instruction is on her tongue."

Her voice had weight because she wasn't operating in the reactive chaos of survival mode.

She didn't speak from anxiety or people-pleasing or the need to prove herself. She spoke from a place of deep rootedness. She moved with the kind of precision and discernment that comes from living an examined, intentional life.

Her wisdom wasn't theoretical. It was earned. It was lived. And it was shared generously—but only after she had first embodied it herself.

She Was Honored (31:28-31)

"Her children arise and call her blessed; her husband also, and he praises her... Give her the reward she has earned, and let her works bring her praise at the city gate."

This woman wasn't honored because she martyred herself. She was honored because she lived with such integrity, such strength, such sovereignty that her life became a testimony.

Her family called her blessed—not because she gave them everything at the expense of herself, but because she modeled what it looks like to live whole.

She built a legacy. Not a legacy of depletion, but a legacy of wisdom, stewardship, and embodied strength.

What She WASN'T

Let's be clear about what the Proverbs 31 woman was not, because this is where culture has distorted her the most:

✗ She wasn't martyring herself. She wasn't giving everything away until she was empty.

✗ She wasn't depleted or burned out. Her strength wasn't the kind that comes from pushing through exhaustion. It was the kind that comes from rest and proper stewardship.

✗ She wasn't performing strength. She didn't have to prove she was capable. She simply was strong—because she had built a life that made strength sustainable.

✗ She wasn't sacrificing her body for others. She honored her temple. Her physical strength was evidence of that.

✗ She wasn't afraid of the future because she had done the work to prepare for it.

✗ She wasn't exhausted. She was embodied. Fully present. Fully alive. Fully sovereign.

THAT'S the Woman I'm Becoming. THAT'S Who I Help You Become.

This is the woman I'm choosing at 57. Not the exhausted martyr. Not the woman who gives until there's nothing left. Not the woman who wears depletion like a badge.

I'm choosing the woman who:
- Builds businesses that serve her life instead of consuming it
- Honors her body as a temple and moves with embodied strength

- Protects her peace with the same fierceness she once used to serve others

- Laughs at the future because she's prepared, not because she's lucky

- Speaks with wisdom earned through survival and stewardship

- Creates a legacy that outlives her

This is the Proverbs 31 woman reimagined. Not as a cautionary tale of how much you should be doing, but as a blueprint for how to live sovereignly, build wisely, and rest deeply.

She had a Sovereign Soft Life built on wise stewardship, not hustle.

And so can you.

The Application: Designing Your Legacy Blueprint

To become *her*, we must stop performing and start embodying. This requires moving from the "Reactive Survival" of our past seasons to the "Proactive Sovereignty" of our future.

THE APPLICATION: Choose Your Entry Point

You don't have to do all of these exercises right now. Choose the one that resonates most deeply with where you are today.

If you're still performing strength instead of embodying it: Start with The Proverbs 31 Embodiment Check

If you're carrying unnecessary weight: Start with The Legacy Blueprint Exercise

If you're ready to envision your sovereign soft life: Start with Vision Exercise: What Does YOUR Proverbs 31 Life Look Like?

If you want to study Scripture with fresh eyes: Start with Scripture Study: The Sovereign Woman

1. The Proverbs 31 Embodiment Check
Review the list below. For each quality, ask yourself: Am I embodying this (it feels natural and restful), or am I performing this (it feels like a heavy mask)?

- Strength (Embodied / Performing)
- Wisdom (Embodied / Performing)
- Business/Productivity (Embodied / Performing)
- Provision for Others (Embodied / Performing)
- Dignity (Embodied / Performing)
- Freedom from Fear (Embodied / Performing)
- Laughter at the Future (Embodied / Performing)

For the ones you marked "Performing," ask yourself:

- Why am I performing this instead of embodying it?

- What would it look like to embody this from a place of rest instead of pressure?

- What would I need to release in order to move from performance to embodiment?

Write your reflections. Be honest. This isn't about shame—it's about clarity.

2. The Legacy Blueprint Exercise
If your life was "clothed in strength and dignity" (Proverbs 31:25) starting tomorrow, what would you immediately stop doing?

What unnecessary weight would you drop?

Write down three things you will no longer carry so that you can make room for your own becoming:

1. _____

2. _____

3. _____

For each one, write one sentence about why you're releasing it and what you're making space for instead.

Example:

"I will no longer carry the belief that rest is selfish. I'm releasing this so I can make space for Sabbath as the foundation of my week, not something I squeeze in when everything else is done."

3. Vision Exercise: What Does YOUR Proverbs 31 Life Look Like?
Close your eyes. Take three deep breaths.

Imagine yourself six months from now in your own "Vegas territory"—your sovereign soft life fully realized.

You are rested. You are running a Kingdom business that honors your Sabbath. You are no longer a sacrifice; you are a sanctuary.

Describe her morning:
- What time does she wake up?
- What's the first thing she does?
- How does her body feel?
- What does she say to herself in the mirror?

Describe her work:
- What is she building?
- Who is she serving?
- How many hours is she working?
- What boundaries protect her peace?

Describe her rest:
- What does her Sabbath look like?

- How does she honor her body?
- What brings her joy?
- How does she laugh at the future?

Write this vision down. Not as a fantasy, but as a blueprint. Because what you can see, you can build.

4. Scripture Study: The Sovereign Woman
Read Proverbs 31:10-31 again—slowly, carefully.

But this time, underline every verse that points to her ownership of her time, her body, and her resources.

Notice:

- How she considers a field before buying it (verse 16) — She doesn't move reactively

- How she sets about her work vigorously (verse 17) — She moves with intention

- How she sees that her trading is profitable (verse 18) — She's financially wise

- How she is clothed with strength and dignity (verse 25) — She doesn't wear exhaustion

- How she can laugh at the days to come (verse 25) — She's prepared, not afraid

- How she speaks with wisdom (verse 26) — Her voice has weight

- How her works bring her praise (verse 31) — She's honored for her stewardship

Notice how she doesn't ask permission to be powerful. She simply is.

This is your model. Not the exhausted martyr. Not the woman who gives until she's empty.

The sovereign woman. The embodied woman. The woman who laughs at the future because she has built a life worth protecting.

The Invitation

You don't have to be the exhausted version of the Proverbs 31 woman.

You don't have to wear depletion like a badge. You don't have to prove your worth by how much you can carry. You don't have to sacrifice your body on the altar of everyone else's expectations.

You can be the woman Scripture actually describes:

Strong. Wise. Prepared. Dignified. Free from fear. Laughing at the future.

You can build the Sovereign Soft Life—a Kingdom-aligned existence where your body is a temple, your business serves your life, and your legacy is one of embodied strength, not exhausted sacrifice.

This is who the Proverbs 31 woman was. This is who I'm becoming at 57. And this is who you're invited to become.

Not someday. Not when everything is perfect. Not when you've finally "earned" the right to rest.

Now.

Because the woman you're becoming? She's been waiting for you to choose her.

In Part III, we'll move from the model (the Proverbs 31 woman) to the practical frameworks that make sovereignty sustainable. We'll explore what the Sovereign Soft Life actually looks like in practice—how to remove unnecessary weight, how to build Sabbath as the architecture of your week, and how to create Kingdom businesses that serve your life instead of consuming it.

The cocoon has broken open. The warrior is awake. The Proverbs 31 blueprint is clear.

Now it's time to build.

You are not too late. You are exactly on time.

> **REMEMBER THIS**
>
> - The Proverbs 31 woman wasn't exhausted—she was EMBODIED.
> - She built from overflow, not depletion.
> - Her strength came from stewarding her temple, not sacrificing it.
> - She could laugh at the future because she was prepared, not lucky.
> - This is my model: strong, sovereign, and building from rest.
> - I am becoming her—not the cultural caricature, but the embodied original..

PART III:
THE SOVEREIGN SOFT LIFE
(The Framework)

I've been in a cocoon for sixteen years—wrapped in caregiving, grief, and survival.

But now, at 57, standing in my Las Vegas sanctuary with the desert sky stretched impossibly wide above me, I'm learning something I've never known: what it actually means to be *soft*.

Not soft because someone else is carrying my weight.

Soft because I've finally put down the weight that was never mine to carry.

Not soft because I'm being taken care of.

Soft because I've learned to take care of myself without depletion.

Not soft because life suddenly got easy.

Soft because I've built a life that doesn't require hardness to survive.

This is Part III: the frameworks that make sovereignty sustainable.

Here, you'll discover what the Sovereign Soft Life actually looks like in practice—how to remove unnecessary weight, how to build Sabbath as the foundation of your week (not an afterthought), and how to create Kingdom businesses that serve your life instead of consuming it.

This isn't theory. This is architecture.

These are the blueprints I'm using to build a life worth protecting—a life where my body is a temple, rest is holy, and my business funds my legacy without stealing my peace.

The cocoon is breaking open. You've learned *who* you're becoming (Part I) and *how* to embody her (Part II).

Now it's time to build the framework that makes sovereignty sustainable.

Welcome to the Sovereign Soft Life.

Chapter 7: DEFINING THE SOVEREIGN SOFT LIFE

"Come to me, all you who are weary and burdened, and I will give you rest. Take my yoke upon you and learn from me, for I am gentle and humble in heart, and you will find rest for your souls. For my yoke is easy and my burden is light."

- Matthew 11:28-30

The Story: Reclaiming the Narrative

If you spend more than five minutes on social media, you will likely encounter the "Soft Life" movement.

In its secular iteration, it is often presented as a performance of luxury: silk robes, expensive vacations, and the controversial "hypergamy" trend—the idea that a woman's softness is bought and paid for by a man who funds her lifestyle so she never has to lift a finger.

I watched this trend from my sanctuary in Las Vegas, and I felt a holy agitation.

Not jealousy. Not judgment. But a deep, spiritual knowing that something sacred had been hijacked and repackaged as something shallow.

Because here's what I knew at 57, after surviving three bouts of sepsis and sixteen years of high-stakes caregiving: The world's version of "soft" is a performance. The Kingdom version of "soft" is a posture.

To the world, "soft" means pampered. It means being taken care of because you are too delicate to handle life. It means outsourcing your strength to someone else's wallet.

But I didn't need someone to fund my lifestyle. I needed a lifestyle that didn't require me to become a weapon or a workhorse just to survive the day.

My discovery of what "soft" really means didn't happen at a spa or on a luxury vacation. It happened in the quiet, ordinary moments of my transition from Savannah to Vegas.

It happened when I realized that for sixteen years, I had been hard.

I had to be. Hardness was my armor. It was the only way to carry the weight of a dying husband, a struggling business, a mother who needed full-time care, and a body that kept trying to quit on me.

Hardness was how I survived.

But once the battle was over—once I'd made my Sacred Exit, once I'd crossed into Vegas, once the emergency room was finally in the rearview mirror—I realized something terrifying:

I was still wearing the armor. And it was crushing the life out of me.

I didn't know how to take it off. I didn't know how to be soft without feeling vulnerable. I didn't know how to rest without feeling guilty. I didn't know how to prioritize myself without hearing the voices of everyone who needed me echoing in my mind.

But in the stillness of my Vegas sanctuary, God began to teach me something I'd never understood before:

Softness isn't weakness. Softness is the fruit of strength rightly applied.

The Sovereign Soft Life isn't about finding someone to carry your weight. It's about having the Kingdom authority to finally put the unnecessary weight down.

It is the absence of friction. It is the realization that I am a daughter of the King, and because I am His, I am authorized—commanded, even—to be gentle with myself.

This is what I'm teaching. Not the Instagram version. Not the "find a rich man" version.

The Kingdom version. The Proverbs 31 version. The sovereign version.

The Concept: Softness as the Absence of Friction

Let's be clear: Softness is not weakness.

In fact, it takes immense strength to be soft in a world that demands you stay hard.

You know what I'm talking about. The world rewards hardness. It praises the woman who "does it all" without complaining. It applauds the woman who pushes through exhaustion, who ignores her body's warning signs, who sacrifices her peace on the altar of productivity.

The world calls that woman "strong."

But I call her what she really is: depleted.

True softness—Kingdom softness, sovereign softness—is what happens when you've removed the unnecessary friction from your life. When you've set boundaries that protect your peace. When you've built a life that doesn't require you to be hard just to survive it.

Here's what softness is NOT:

✗ You are NOT soft because someone else carries the weight. You are soft because you have used your sovereignty to decide which weights are yours to carry and which are unnecessary friction.

✗ You are NOT soft because you are being taken care of. You are soft because you have learned to take care of yourself without depletion.

✗ You are NOT soft because life is suddenly easy. Life will always have its seasons of trial. You are soft because you have built a life that does not require hardness to survive.

Here's what softness IS:

☑ Softness is the removal of unnecessary weight.

☑ Softness is the fruit of wise stewardship.

☑ Softness is what happens when your life is aligned with Kingdom principles—Sabbath rest, embodied strength, protected peace.

☑ Softness is the hum of a well-oiled life—powerful, but without grinding.

Think of a high-performance engine. When it is well-oiled and perfectly aligned, it moves with a soft hum. There's no grinding. No friction. No parts wearing each other down.

That engine is still powerful. It's still doing the work. But it's doing it from a place of alignment, not exhaustion.

That's what I want for you. A life where the grinding stops.

A life where you're still strong, still capable, still productive—but you're no longer wearing yourself down in the process.

That's the Sovereign Soft Life.

The Three Pillars of the Sovereign Soft Life

To live this way, we must build on three non-negotiable pillars. These aren't optional. They're not "nice to have." They're the foundation.

Pillar 1: Body as Temple
We stop treating our bodies as tools for serving others and start treating them with reverence.

Your body is the vessel for your calling. If the vessel is cracked and exhausted, the calling is compromised.

In the Sovereign Soft Life, physical health is not a vanity project. It's not about fitting into a certain size or looking a certain way. It's a stewardship requirement.

You cannot build a legacy if your body gives out before you're done. You cannot serve from overflow if your body is running on fumes. You cannot teach others to honor their temples if you're still treating yours like a warehouse.

Body as Temple means:
- Your body gets rest before anyone else's needs get met
- Your health is a priority, not an afterthought
- You move your body with intention, not punishment
- You feed your body with nourishment, not just convenience
- You honor your body's limits instead of pushing past them

This is what the Proverbs 31 woman modeled. Her arms were strong (31:17) because she stewarded her body well. She didn't deplete herself. She built from overflow.

Pillar 2: Rest as Holy
In our culture, rest is treated as a reward for a job well done. In the Kingdom, rest is a commandment.

Sabbath isn't what we do when we're finished. It's the sacred practice that fuels our beginning. It's the foundation upon which the other six days are built.

This is what I finally learned in Vegas: Sabbath isn't optional. It's architectural.

The other six days of your week are only as strong as the foundation of your Sabbath. If you skip rest, if you treat it as negotiable, everything else starts to crumble.

Rest as Holy means:

- Sabbath is a 24-hour perimeter around your peace (Friday sundown to Saturday sundown)
- You design your business to honor rest, not violate it
- You say no to anything that crosses your Sabbath boundary
- You teach others that your rest is non-negotiable
- You model for your family, your clients, your community that rest is worship

This is countercultural. This will make people uncomfortable. But it's Kingdom.

Pillar 3: Business as Service (Not Consumption)
We reject the "hustle" culture that demands we sacrifice our sleep, our peace, and our families for a profit margin.

We build businesses—like the Proverbs 31 woman—that serve our life, fund our legacy, and respect our boundaries.

The Proverbs 31 woman was a strategic entrepreneur. She considered fields and bought them. She planted vineyards. She made linen garments and sold them. She understood wealth-building.

But here's what she didn't do: She didn't hustle herself into the ground.

She built a business that aligned with her values. That honored her household. That allowed her to be clothed in strength and dignity, not exhaustion.

Business as Service means:

- Your business funds your life; it doesn't consume it
- You design your offerings to honor Sabbath (no weekend work, no emergency availability)
- You work from overflow, not depletion
- You say no to opportunities that violate your peace
- You build for legacy, not just survival

This is what I'm building now. Private advisory. Cohorts. Masterclasses. Digital products. Retreats. All of it designed to serve my life, honor my Sabbath, and protect my peace.

What the Sovereign Soft Life Means for You
Living as a Chief Legacy Architect—a sovereign woman building the soft life—means embodying these truths daily:

☑ My body is a temple—treated as sacred, not as a tool.

☑ Rest is holy—Sabbath isn't optional, it's commanded.

☑ Soft doesn't mean weak—it means I am strong enough to be gentle with myself.

☑ I'm a woman of God AND I prioritize myself (because I cannot pour from an empty cup).

☑ Embodiment = being fully present in a body that's healed, rested, and powerful.

☑ I build businesses that SERVE my life instead of consuming it.

This is not a "lifestyle brand." This is not about aesthetics or performance.

This is Kingdom living. This is the Proverbs 31 model reimagined for the modern woman who is ready to stop performing and start being.

This is what happens when you remove the unnecessary weight, honor your Sabbath, and build from a place of embodied sovereignty.

This is the Sovereign Soft Life.

The Application: Designing Your Softness

THE APPLICATION: Choose Your Entry Point

You don't have to do all of these exercises right now. Choose the one that feels most urgent for where you are today.

If you're carrying unnecessary weight: Start with The Weight Audit

If you're ready to design your sovereign soft life: Start with Soft Life Design

If you need to examine your relationship with hardness: Start with Reflection Questions

1. The Weight Audit
Look at your current daily schedule—not the ideal version, but the real one.

Identify three things you are doing out of "habitual hardness"—things you do because you feel you must, or because you've always done them, but they create friction in your soul.

These might be:
- Obligations you've been carrying out of guilt, not calling
- Relationships that drain you more than they fill you
- Business tasks that could be automated, delegated, or eliminated
- "Should" statements that aren't actually aligned with your values
- Perfectionist standards that no one but you cares about

For each one, ask:
- What unnecessary weight am I carrying?
- Why am I still carrying it? (Fear? Guilt? Habit? People-pleasing?)
- What would happen if I simply put it down?

Write down your three weights. Then write one sentence for each about what you're releasing and why.

Example:

"I'm releasing the obligation to attend every family gathering. I've been carrying this out of guilt, not genuine desire. If I put it down, I'll have energy for the relationships that actually fill me."

2. Soft Life Design
Forget the Instagram version of the soft life—the silk robes and champagne brunches.

Describe YOUR Sovereign Soft Life.

Answer these questions:

If there was no friction in your morning, what would it look like?
- What time would you wake up?
- What would be the first thing you do?
- How would your body feel?
- What wouldn't be there (emails, obligations, chaos)?

If your business served your life instead of consuming it, how many hours would you work?
- What days would be work days?

- What days would be sacred rest?
- What boundaries would protect your peace?
- What revenue streams would honor your Sabbath?

What does your body feel like when it is treated as a sanctuary?
- How would you move differently?
- How would you eat differently?
- How would you rest differently?
- What would you no longer tolerate?

Write this out in detail. Not as a fantasy, but as a blueprint. Because what you can see clearly, you can build intentionally.

3. Reflection Questions

Take out your journal. Answer these questions with radical honesty:

Where are you choosing "hardness" as a defense mechanism?

Are you staying hard because you're afraid that if you soften, people will take advantage of you? Are you afraid that softness equals weakness?

Do you believe you are "allowed" to be soft without a man or a circumstance "earning" it for you?

Do you believe you deserve rest, peace, and gentleness simply because you are a daughter of the King? Or do you believe you have to earn it through performance, productivity, or being "taken care of" by someone else?

What is one boundary you can set this week to protect your "Sacred Architecture"?

What's one thing you can say no to that will create more space for softness? What's one weight you can put down that will reduce the friction?

Write it down. Be specific. Then do it.

The Invitation to Softness

You don't have to stay hard.

You don't have to keep wearing the armor long after the battle is over. You don't have to prove your strength by how much weight you can carry or how much pain you can endure.

Softness is not weakness. Softness is wisdom.

It's the wisdom to know which battles are yours and which are not. It's the wisdom to remove unnecessary friction. It's the wisdom to build a life that honors your temple, protects your Sabbath, and serves your legacy.

The Sovereign Soft Life isn't about being pampered or taken care of. It's about being stewarded by yourself, for yourself, in alignment with Kingdom principles.

It's about finally—after years of hardness—giving yourself permission to be gentle.

Not because someone earned it for you. Not because life suddenly got easy.

But because you are a daughter of the King, and He commanded you to rest.

In the next chapter, we'll explore the philosophy that shaped how I think about sovereign living: the P.R.I.V.É. framework. It's not the center of my work, but it's part of my foundation—a tool I carry from the chapter of Suite Life Privé that taught me about precision, refinement, and visionary living.

The Sovereign Soft Life is not a trend. It's a Kingdom practice. And you are worthy of it—not someday, but today.

You are not too late. You are exactly on time.

REMEMBER THIS

- Soft doesn't mean weak—it means I've removed unnecessary weight.
- The three pillars: Body as Temple, Rest as Holy, Business as Service.
- Softness is the absence of friction, not the absence of strength.
- I'm building a life that doesn't require hardness to survive.
- This is Kingdom living—Proverbs 31 for modern women.
- The Sovereign Soft Life is not a trend. It's a Kingdom practice.

Chapter 8:
THE P.R.I.V.É. PHILOSOPHY

"But everything should be done in a fitting and orderly way."

- 1 Corinthians 14:40

The Story: Lessons from the Suite Life

Every architect has a period where they hone their craft on specific structures before they are ready to design a cathedral. For me, that season was *Suite Life Privé*.

During my transition—as I moved from the weight of caregiving in Savannah toward the desert clarity of Las Vegas—I founded a boutique hospitality and lifestyle brand. It was born out of my background in luxury service and my deep need to see beauty and order in a world that had felt chaotic for far too long.

Through Suite Life Privé and its Collective, I wasn't just building a business; I was teaching myself how to live with intentionality again.

I needed to see that life could be curated, not just survived. I needed to remember that details mattered, that beauty was healing, that excellence was possible even after loss. Suite Life Privé was my practice ground for re-entering the world—not as Survival Karen, but as a woman who could create spaces of beauty and order.

It was during this time that I developed the P.R.I.V.É. framework. At the time, I thought it was purely about luxury hospitality and high-end lifestyle design. But as I leaned into my calling as an embodiment coach and advisor, I realized that God was giving me a language for *sovereignty*.

The framework I'd created to curate exceptional experiences for others was actually teaching me how to curate my own life. How to move with precision instead of chaos. How to choose refinement over convenience. How to build for legacy instead of just survival.

Suite Life Privé served its purpose beautifully. It was the bridge that carried me from "Survival Karen" to the woman I am today. It taught me about design, intention, and what it means to live with distinction. While my work has now shifted toward deep embodiment and Kingdom legacy, the P.R.I.V.É. philosophy remains part of my foundation.

It is the lens through which I view excellence, stewardship, and the design of a life. It isn't the center of my work anymore, but it is the precision-tool I use to build it.

This is what I want you to understand: Your past seasons aren't wasted. They're formative. Suite Life Privé wasn't a failure because I'm not doing that work anymore. It was a necessary chapter that shaped how I think, how I move, and how I build.

And the P.R.I.V.É. framework? It's now woven into everything I teach about the Sovereign Soft Life.

The P.R.I.V.É. Framework for Sovereign Living

To live a Sovereign Soft Life, you cannot be haphazard. You must be an architect. The P.R.I.V.É. framework is how we move from the "accidental life" of survival to the "designed life" of sovereignty.

P — PRECISION: The Death of Randomness
In the world of high-luxury, nothing is an accident. Every scent, every fabric, every second of timing is curated with intention.

Nothing happens by default. Everything is chosen.

In your Sovereign Soft Life: Precision means clarity. It is the intentional design of your calendar, your boundaries, and your business systems. It is knowing exactly what you are saying "yes" to and, more importantly, exactly why you are saying "no."

Precision is what allows you to move with confidence instead of chaos. It's what keeps you from being reactive, from constantly putting out fires, from living at the mercy of everyone else's urgency.

Precision in practice looks like:

- A morning routine that's intentionally designed, not cobbled together
- A business structure that protects your Sabbath by design, not by luck
- Boundaries that are clear and communicated, not assumed and violated
- A calendar that reflects your priorities, not just everyone else's demands
- Systems that reduce friction instead of creating it

When you live with precision, you stop wasting energy on unnecessary chaos. You stop second-guessing yourself. You stop reacting to every crisis as if it's your emergency to solve.

Precision creates softness. Because when your life is intentionally designed, you're not constantly grinding against resistance.

R — REFINED EXPERIENCES: Quality Over Convenience
Most women live lives of convenience—eating what's available, working when asked, and taking whatever "rest" is left over.

We default to convenience because it requires less thought, less effort, less planning. But convenience comes at a cost. It depletes us. It keeps us in survival mode. It robs us of the richness that comes from intentional living.

In your Sovereign Soft Life: We choose refinement. We curate experiences that transcend the mundane. We prioritize quality over quantity in our relationships, our work, and our environment.

Refinement isn't about being pretentious or expensive. It's about being *intentional*. It's about asking: "Does this align with the rhythm of the woman I am becoming?"

Refinement in practice looks like:

- Choosing one nourishing meal over three convenient ones
- Designing your workspace to feel like a sanctuary, not a storage closet
- Selecting clients who align with your values, not just your revenue needs
- Spending time with people who fill you, not drain you
- Creating rituals that feel sacred, not rushed

Refinement is the difference between grabbing whatever's in the fridge and sitting down to a meal that actually nourishes your body. It's the difference between answering every email immediately and setting aside intentional time to respond with clarity.

Refinement creates dignity. Because when you honor yourself with quality experiences, you stop accepting scraps.

I — IMMERSIVE LUXURY: Embodied Presence
Society tells us luxury is something you buy. I tell you luxury is something you *are*.

The world's version of luxury is external: designer labels, expensive vacations, champagne brunches. But Kingdom luxury—*true* luxury—is internal. It's the richness of a rested soul. The wealth of a quiet mind. The abundance of a body that feels like a sanctuary.

In your Sovereign Soft Life: Immersive luxury is the ability to be fully present, fully embodied, and fully alive in the moment. It's not about material consumption; it's about the depth of your experience.

This is what I discovered in my Vegas sanctuary: the most luxurious thing I could do wasn't buy expensive things. It was to finally *be present in my own body*.

Immersive luxury in practice looks like:

- Sitting on the edge of your bed in the morning and actually feeling your feet on the floor
- Tasting your food instead of eating while distracted
- Walking without your phone and noticing the sky
- Being in a conversation without planning what you'll say next
- Resting without guilt, without checking your to-do list, without apologizing

Immersive luxury is what happens when you stop performing and start *being*. When you stop dissociating from your body and start inhabiting it. When you stop rushing through life and start actually living it.

Immersive luxury is embodiment. And embodiment is the foundation of the Sovereign Soft Life.

V — VISIONARY LIVING: Designing for Longevity
Survival mode only looks at the next hour. Visionary living looks at the next decade.

For sixteen years, I lived in survival mode. I couldn't think past the next medication dose, the next crisis, the next thing that needed to be handled. I was in a perpetual state of emergency response.

But visionary living requires you to lift your head and ask: "If I keep living this way, what will my life look like in ten years? Twenty years? When I'm 70?"

In your Sovereign Soft Life: We stop building for immediate fires and start building for legacy. We design for the woman we will be at 70 and 80. We make decisions based on our future sovereignty, not our current exhaustion.

Visionary living is what the Proverbs 31 woman modeled. She planted vineyards (31:16)—crops that take years to produce fruit. She wasn't thinking about next week's revenue. She was thinking generationally.

Visionary living in practice looks like:

- Building a business that can scale without consuming more of your time
- Investing in your health now so you're strong at 70
- Creating systems that protect your peace long-term, not just today
- Making financial decisions that honor your future self
- Saying no to opportunities that would deplete your body or violate your Sabbath—even if they're lucrative right now

Visionary living requires you to think like a steward, not a survivor. It requires you to ask: "Is this decision aligned with the woman I'm becoming, or is it just solving today's crisis?"

Visionary living creates legacy. Because you're no longer just reacting—you're architecting.

É — ÉLAN & EXCELLENCE: Kingdom Distinction

Élan is a French word for energy, style, and enthusiasm. It's a refined presence that doesn't require loud performance. It's the quiet confidence of someone who knows who they are.

In your Sovereign Soft Life: We move with grace and mastery. We reject the "hustle" and instead embrace "distinction." We do fewer things, but we do them with a timeless quality that reflects the excellence of the Kingdom.

This is what I mean when I say you don't need to do more—you need to do what you do *with distinction*.

The world tells us to hustle harder, do more, be everywhere, say yes to everything. But élan says: "I move with intention. I do what I do exceptionally well. And I don't apologize for what I choose not to do."

Élan & Excellence in practice looks like:

- Offering three exceptional services instead of ten mediocre ones
- Writing one powerful email instead of ten scattered posts
- Showing up fully present in one conversation instead of half-present in five
- Building one signature program that transforms lives instead of chasing every trend
- Moving through your day with grace instead of frantic energy

Élan is what makes the Sovereign Soft Life sustainable. Because you're not trying to be everything to everyone. You're being *exactly who you are* with clarity and confidence.

Élan creates authority. Because people recognize mastery when they see it.

The Foundation, Not the Destination

I share this framework with you because it is how I think. It is the "Sacred Architecture" of my mind.

You don't need to become a luxury hospitality expert to use these tools. You simply need to realize that your life is a high-value asset that deserves to be managed with the same precision as a five-star estate.

P.R.I.V.É. taught me that I could take the fragments of a life broken by grief and sepsis and assemble them into something distinguished and powerful. It was the practice ground for my sovereignty.

And now I'm teaching you the same principles—not so you can build a hospitality brand, but so you can build a life worth protecting.

The Application: The P.R.I.V.É. Life Audit

THE APPLICATION: Choose Your Entry Point

You don't have to do all of these exercises right now. Choose the one that feels most relevant to where you are today.

If your life feels chaotic: Start with The Precision vs. Chaos Check

If you're settling for convenience over quality: Start with The Refinement Practice

If you're building for today instead of tomorrow: Start with Visionary Design Exercise

If you're not sure which principle you need most: Start with Reflection Question

1. The Precision vs. Chaos Check
Where in your life is there "unnecessary friction" because of a lack of precision?

Look at these areas:

- Your morning routine: Is it intentional or reactive?
- Your client onboarding: Is it smooth or chaotic?
- Your boundaries: Are they clear or constantly being violated?
- Your calendar: Does it reflect your priorities or everyone else's urgency?

Identify one area where "Precision" would immediately create "Softness."

Write down:

- What's currently chaotic?
- What intentional structure would eliminate that chaos?
- What's one thing you can design this week to create more precision?

Example:

"My mornings are chaotic because I check my phone immediately and respond to everyone else's needs before I've even felt my own body. I'm going to design a precise morning ritual: feet on floor, five breaths, embodiment practice, THEN phone. This precision will create softness by protecting my peace before the day begins."

2. The Refinement Practice

Choose one area of your life this week—perhaps your evening routine or your workspace—and curate it with intention.

Remove the clutter. Add one element of beauty. Experience the shift from "convenience" to "refinement."

Example areas to refine:

- Your workspace: Clear the surface. Add one plant or candle. Make it feel like a sanctuary.

- Your evening wind-down: Replace scrolling with a book. Replace rushed chaos with intentional transition.

- Your meals: Replace grab-and-go with one sit-down, nourishing meal this week.

Refinement isn't about perfection. It's about intention.

After you've refined this one area, journal:

- How did it feel different?

- What friction was removed?

- How can you apply this principle to other areas?

3. Visionary Design Exercise

Look at your current business or work-life. If you continue at this exact pace and style for the next ten years, what will your health and spirit look like at 67?

Be brutally honest:

- Will your body still be strong, or will it be broken?

- Will your peace still be intact, or will you be burned out?

- Will you have built a legacy, or just survived another decade?

What visionary adjustment needs to be made *today* to ensure the woman you become is sovereign and strong?

Write down:

- One thing you need to STOP doing (even if it's profitable right now)

- One thing you need to START doing (even if it feels uncomfortable)
- One boundary you need to SET to protect your future sovereignty

This isn't about guilt. This is about stewardship.

4. Reflection Question
Which of the five P.R.I.V.É. principles feels the most foreign to you right now? Why?

- **Precision** — Do you resist structure because you fear it will feel rigid?
- **Refinement** — Do you default to convenience because intentionality feels like "too much"?
- **Immersive Luxury** — Do you struggle to be present because you're always thinking ahead?
- **Visionary Living** — Do you only think short-term because long-term feels overwhelming?
- **Élan & Excellence** — Do you do too much because you're afraid of being "not enough"?

The one you resist is usually the one you need most to bridge the gap to your becoming.

Journal about it. Ask yourself: What am I afraid will happen if I embrace this principle?

Then ask: What becomes possible if I do?

The Truth About Your Foundation

Suite Life Privé wasn't a detour. It was preparation.

The P.R.I.V.É. framework isn't just about luxury hospitality. It's about sovereign living.

And the woman you're becoming? She moves with precision, refinement, presence, vision, and distinction—not because she's performing, but because she's embodied.

This is the foundation. The next chapter will show you how to build on it with the most non-negotiable element of the Sovereign Soft Life: Sabbath as Architecture.

Because precision without rest is just another form of hustle. And we're done with that.

You are not too late. You are exactly on time.

Chapter 9:
SABBATH AS ARCHITECTURE

"Remember the Sabbath day by keeping it holy. Six days you shall labor and do all your work, but the seventh day is a sabbath to the LORD your God."
- Exodus 20:8-10

The Story: Building from the Foundation

For years, I treated my faith like a beautiful piece of art—I hung it on the walls of my life, but it didn't really change the floor plan.

I would work myself to the point of collapse, and then on Sunday (or whatever day I could spare), I would collapse into a pew and call it "rest." I would drag my exhausted body to church, sit through a service while my mind raced through my to-do list, and then rush home to get back to caregiving, business deadlines, and the endless cycle of survival.

I called that Sabbath. But it wasn't rest. It was just a different location for my exhaustion.

I was trying to fit my faith into my business. I was trying to squeeze God into the margins of a schedule that was already bursting at the seams with caregiving, sepsis recovery, and the relentless "hustle" of trying to stay afloat.

It didn't work. It will never work.

For sixteen years, I operated under the same lie that so many Kingdom women believe: **"If I work hard enough, God will bless my effort. If I sacrifice enough, He'll honor my devotion."**

But here's what I learned the hard way: God doesn't bless disobedience. And ignoring the Sabbath commandment—no matter how "good" my reasons—is disobedience.

I wasn't honoring God by working seven days a week. I was essentially telling Him: *"I don't trust You to keep the world spinning for 24 hours without my help."*

It was only when I moved to Las Vegas—when I finally had the space to breathe, when the emergency room was finally in the rearview mirror—that I had an epiphany:

I had been trying to build a Kingdom life on a survival-mode foundation.

And you can't build something sacred on a foundation of chaos.

I finally figured out how to honor God and the Sabbath in my work. It wasn't by doing more "faith-based" marketing or adding a fish symbol to my business card. It wasn't by reading my Bible during my lunch break or praying between caregiving tasks.

It was by building my business FROM my faith, not around it.

I stopped asking God to bless my busy schedule and started asking Him to show me His architecture for time.

I realized that if I was going to call myself a Sovereign woman, I had to submit to the Sovereign's schedule.

And His schedule includes rest. Not as an afterthought. Not as a reward. But as a **commandment**. As the **foundation** upon which everything else is built.

The Teaching: The Foundation, Not the Day Off

Sabbath Is Not What You Think It Is

In our culture, we view rest as a reward for a job well done. We think, *"If I check everything off my list, then I have earned the right to sit down."*

But in the Kingdom, Sabbath is not a day off. **It is the foundation the other six days sit on.**

Think about it: In Genesis, God rested on the seventh day—not because He was tired, but to **establish a rhythm**. He modeled rest as part of the creative order. Rest wasn't the absence of work; it was the completion of work.

And when God gave the Ten Commandments, the Sabbath wasn't a suggestion. It was the fourth commandment:

"Remember the Sabbath day by keeping it holy. Six days you shall labor and do all your work, but the seventh day is a sabbath to the Lord your God." (Exodus 20:8-10)

Remember. Not "if you have time." Not "when you're finished."

Remember. The Sabbath is a memorial—a weekly reminder that you are not the one holding the world together. God is.

But here's where most of us get it wrong: We treat Sabbath as something we "squeeze in" after the work is finished. We think of it as the period at the end of the sentence.

But Sabbath is actually the foundation upon which the sentence is built.

When you honor Sabbath first—when you place that 24-hour perimeter of rest on your calendar before anything else—the other six days arrange themselves around it. Your work becomes more focused. Your boundaries become clearer. Your peace becomes non-negotiable.

But when you treat Sabbath as optional, everything else becomes urgent. Your calendar fills with chaos. Your body stays in survival mode. And your spirit forgets what it feels like to be still.

The Architecture of Time

In architecture, the foundation determines what can be built on top of it. If the foundation is weak, the structure will crumble—no matter how beautiful the design.

The same is true for your life.

If you try to build a Kingdom business, a sovereign life, or embodied strength on a foundation of chronic depletion, it will collapse. Maybe not today. Maybe not next month. But eventually, your body will stop you. Your peace will be gone. Your spirit will be exhausted.

Sabbath is the foundation that keeps everything else standing.

For me, this architecture is non-negotiable: **Friday sundown through Saturday sundown.** This is my 24-hour sanctuary. During these hours, I am not a "Chief Legacy Architect." I am not a coach. I am not an author. I am not checking email, posting on social media, or managing anything.

I am simply a daughter of the King.

The revolutionary act of not being available—to clients, to social media, to the "grind"—is the ultimate expression of my sovereignty.

When I am unavailable to the world, I am fully available to my soul.

And here's what I've discovered: The other six days don't fall apart when I rest for one. In fact, they get better. My clarity improves. My creativity flows. My body feels stronger. My decisions are wiser.

Because I'm no longer running on fumes. I'm building from overflow.

The Lie of "I Can't Afford to Rest"

I know what you're thinking. I thought the same thing for years:

"I can't afford to take a full day off. I have too much to do. People need me. My business will suffer. I'll fall behind."

But here's the truth: **You can't afford NOT to rest.**

Every time you skip Sabbath, you're making a withdrawal from your body, your peace, and your future. And eventually, the account runs dry.

I learned this the hard way. Three times, my body shut down completely because I refused to honor rest. Three times, sepsis forced me into a hospital bed where I had no choice but to stop.

God will get your attention one way or another. You can choose to rest willingly, or your body will force you to rest eventually.

Sabbath is not a luxury. It's survival.

And for the woman building the Sovereign Soft Life? It's not just survival—it's the **architecture** that makes sovereignty sustainable.

Your Design Filter: Protecting the Perimeter

To live the Sovereign Soft Life, you must treat **peace as a design constraint, not a reward.**

This is how I approach every business decision now. When I design a new offering—like the *Becoming Her* ebook, my private advisory, or a masterclass—I run it through my **Sabbath Filter**:

The Sabbath Filter: Three Questions

1. Is it emergency-responsive?
If a business model requires me to be "on call" to put out fires 24/7, it doesn't fit my architecture.

I don't offer services that require me to be available at all hours. I don't work with clients who expect me to respond on weekends. I don't build businesses that demand my constant presence.

2. Does it respect the weekend?
I do not host events, calls, or obligations from Friday evening through Saturday sundown.

My weekends are **protected, not event-dependent.**

This means no Saturday workshops. No Saturday speaking engagements. No "quick calls" on Friday night. My Sabbath is sacred, and I design my business to honor that.

3. Is it built to honor rest?
I choose business models that allow the work to move while I am still.

- **Digital products** (ebooks, guides) that people can purchase anytime
- **Recorded masterclasses** that don't require me to be live
- **Scheduled advisory calls** that happen Monday-Thursday
- **Cohorts** that run on a set schedule with clear boundaries
- **Automated systems** that handle inquiries, payments, and onboarding

This isn't just about "taking a break." **This is about building a business that is Sabbath-compatible by design.**

Because if your business model requires you to violate your Sabbath to succeed, then it's not a Kingdom business. It's a hustle dressed up in faith language.

How to Build Sabbath-Compatible Work

1. Automation as Stewardship
Use technology to protect your peace.

Your automated email sequences, your scheduling systems, your payment processors—these are the "Levites" of your business. They keep the temple running while you are at rest.

This isn't lazy. This is wise.
The Proverbs 31 woman had servants (31:15). She didn't do everything herself. She built systems that allowed her household to run smoothly so she could focus on high-level work—and so she could rest.

You can do the same. Automate what can be automated. Delegate what can be delegated. Protect your Sabbath with the same fierceness you protect your calling.

2. Setting Boundaries Clients Respect
People don't respect your time because you ask them to. They respect it because **you respect it.**

When you are firm about your Sabbath, you actually attract clients who value depth and boundaries. You repel people who want 24/7 access. And that's a good thing.

How to communicate your Sabbath boundaries:

- Include it in your client onboarding: *"I honor Sabbath from Friday sundown through Saturday sundown. I do not check email or respond to messages during this time."*

- Set up an auto-responder for weekend emails: *"I'm observing Sabbath rest and will respond on [day]."*

- Don't apologize for it. Don't explain it. Simply state it as fact.

The right clients will respect it. The wrong clients will self-select out. Either way, your peace is protected.

3. No Weekend Obligations
This is the hardest part for most women. Because we've been conditioned to believe that being "available" is being "valuable."

But here's the truth: **Constant availability is not a virtue. It's a sign of poor boundaries.**

No weekend obligations means:
- No "checking just one email"
- No "quick social media posts"
- No "let me just finish this one thing"
- No working "while the kids are busy"

Once the sun goes down on Friday, the digital door is **locked**.

Your Sabbath is a 24-hour perimeter around your peace. And nothing—no client, no opportunity, no "urgent" request—gets to cross that perimeter.

The Application: Designing Your 24-Hour Sanctuary

THE APPLICATION: Choose Your Entry Point
You don't have to do all of these exercises right now. Choose the one that feels most needed for where you are today.

If you've never honored a full Sabbath: Start with **The 24-Hour Sanctuary Guide**

If you're not sure what rest looks like for you: Start with **Your Sabbath Design**

If your business is violating your rest: Start with **Business Sabbath Audit**

If you're ready to commit: Start with **The 30-Day Sabbath Commitment**

1. The 24-Hour Sanctuary Guide

Choose your 24-hour window. I recommend **Friday sundown to Saturday sundown** to align with the biblical Sabbath, but if another day works better for your rhythm, honor that.

Here's how to structure your first true Sabbath:

Hour 0 (The Closing):

- Turn off your phone (or put it in airplane mode)
- Light a candle
- Say a prayer of transition: *"This is the day the Lord has made. I will rest in it."*

Hours 1–12 (The Deep Rest):

- Sleep without an alarm
- Wake naturally
- Eat something that feels like a gift, not just fuel
- Move slowly through your morning
- No email. No news. No social media.

Hours 13–24 (The Soul Feed):

- Walk outside and notice the sky
- Read something that nourishes you (Scripture, poetry, a book that fills you)
- Pray without a to-do list

- Laugh with family or sit in silence
- Journal if it feels natural
- **No "productive" thoughts allowed**

The Closing (Hour 24):

- Say a prayer of gratitude
- Transition back into the week with clarity and rest

This isn't a rigid schedule. It's a framework. Adjust it to fit your life, but honor the core principle: 24 hours of sacred rest.

2. Your Sabbath Design
What does your ideal Sabbath look like?

Not what you think it "should" look like. Not what someone else's Sabbath looks like. **Yours.**

Answer these questions:

- Does your Sabbath involve silence, or does it involve laughter and conversation?
- Does it involve being alone, or being with loved ones?
- Does it involve cooking a special meal, or ordering in so you don't have to work?
- Does it involve music, nature, art, or simply being still?

Write down three elements that make a day feel "holy" to you.

For me, it's:

1. Sleeping without an alarm
2. A slow breakfast with good coffee

3. Walking in the desert with no agenda

For you, it might be completely different. And that's okay. **Your Sabbath is your sanctuary. Design it accordingly.**

3. Business Sabbath Audit
Where is your work currently violating your rest?

Be brutally honest:

- Do you answer DMs on Saturday morning?
- Do you "just check" your email on Sunday?
- Do you feel guilty when you're not working?
- Do you schedule client calls on weekends "just this once"?
- Do you work on digital products during your "rest" day because "it doesn't feel like work"?

Identify one "leak" in your architecture and plug it this week.

Maybe it's:

- Turning off notifications on weekends
- Setting an auto-responder
- Saying no to a Saturday event
- Deleting work apps from your phone for 24 hours

One leak. One week. Watch what happens.

4. The 30-Day Sabbath Commitment
I challenge you to honor a true, 24-hour Sabbath for the next **four weeks**.

Not because you're tired (though you probably are).

Not because you need a break (though you definitely do).

Do it because you are sovereign. And sovereign women submit to the Sovereign's rhythm.

Here's your commitment:

"For the next 30 days, I will honor a 24-hour Sabbath every week. I will not work, check email, or engage with business during this time. I will rest because God commanded it, and I trust Him to sustain what I've built while I am still."

Sign it. Date it. Put it somewhere you'll see it every day.

Then watch what happens.

Watch how the other six days begin to align themselves with the peace you found in the seventh.

Watch how your body stops living in survival mode.

Watch how your business doesn't fall apart—in fact, it gets stronger because **you're** stronger.

Watch how rest becomes the foundation everything else is built on.

The Truth About Sabbath

Sabbath is not about you being lazy. It's about you being obedient.

Sabbath is not about you "earning" rest. It's about you honoring the rhythm God established at creation.

Sabbath is not a day off. It's the **foundation** your other six days sit on.

And when you finally honor it—when you stop trying to fit your faith into your business and start building your business FROM your faith—everything changes.

Your body stops grinding. Your mind stops racing. Your spirit remembers what it feels like to be still.

And the Sovereign Soft Life? It becomes sustainable. Because you're no longer building on a foundation of depletion. You're building on a foundation of sacred rest.

This is how you honor God in your work: You build your work around His rhythm, not the other way around.

This is Sabbath as architecture. And it's non-negotiable.

In the next chapter, we'll explore what it looks like to build a Kingdom business that actually honors this architecture—a business that serves your life instead of consuming it. Because Sabbath without the right business model is just wishing. But Sabbath WITH a sovereign business structure? That's legacy.

The foundation is set. Now it's time to build.

You are not too late. You are exactly on time.

REMEMBER THIS
<ul><li>Sabbath is the FOUNDATION, not the day off.</li><li>The other six days arrange themselves around my sacred 24 hours.</li><li>I build my business FROM my faith, not around it.</li><li>The Sabbath Filter: Is it emergency-responsive? Does it respect weekends? Does it honor rest?</li><li>God can hold the world together for 24 hours without me.</li><li>My Sabbath is non-negotiable. My peace is worth protecting</li></ul>

Chapter 10:
KINGDOM BUSINESS & THE LAPTOP LIFESTYLE

"She considers a field and buys it; out of her earnings she plants a vineyard... She sees that her trading is profitable, and her lamp does not go out at night."

- Proverbs 31:16, 18

The Story: From Service to Sovereignty

For most of my career, I lived in the world of high-touch hospitality. I was the one ensuring the linens were crisp, the welcome was warm, and every physical need of my guests was met before they even realized they had it. I spent over 25 years in luxury service—managing hotels, curating events, coordinating travel, anticipating needs.

I was good at it. Really good at it.

Through Suite Life Privé and The Collective, I mastered the art of serving others. I could walk into a space and immediately see what was needed. I could read people, anticipate problems, create seamless experiences. I could make someone feel like the most important person in the room.

But there was a cost: I was always serving. Never sovereign.

In hospitality, the guest always comes first. Their comfort. Their needs. Their schedule. Your job is to disappear into the background and make everything run smoothly while remaining invisible.

For years, this felt like my calling. And in many ways, it was—for that season.

But as I transitioned into this new season at 57, I realized that while hospitality was formative, it wasn't my destination.

Those businesses weren't failures—they were the laboratory where I learned how to design environments, anticipate needs, and move with precision. I just didn't realize yet that the most important environment I would ever design was the one inside a woman's soul.

And the most important needs I would ever anticipate weren't physical—they were spiritual and emotional.

Today, my work has shifted from serving physical needs to protecting and empowering a woman's sovereignty.

In hospitality, I was the one behind the scenes making sure the guest was comfortable. In my Kingdom Business Advisory, I am the one standing beside the woman, showing her how to build a perimeter around her own peace so she can lead without losing herself.

I'm no longer the one fixing everything for her. I'm the one teaching her how to architect her own life so she doesn't need constant fixing.

This is the energy shift: I no longer move from a place of *"How can I help you?"* I move from a place of *"How can we architect a life that honors your God-given authority?"*

In hospitality, I served. In this work, I protect and empower.

And that shift—from service to sovereignty—changed everything about how I build my business.

The Strategy: Stewardship Over Hustle

The biggest lie we are told about building a business is that it requires us to trade our health for our wealth.

We are taught that "hustle" is the only way to "scale." That if we're not working 60-80 hours a week, we're not serious. That rest is for people who aren't ambitious. That exhaustion is the price of success.

But "hustle" is just a secular word for "striving." And striving is a lack of trust.

When you're hustling, you're operating from scarcity. You're saying, *"If I don't do this, it won't get done. If I don't push harder, I'll fall behind. If I rest, I'll lose."*

But when you're stewarding, you're operating from abundance. You're saying, *"God gave me this assignment. He will sustain what He called me to build. I can rest because He doesn't."*

Hustle is rooted in fear. Stewardship is rooted in faith.

In the Sovereign Soft Life, we move from time-for-money execution to high-level advisory and thought leadership.

We don't build businesses that consume us. We build businesses that serve our life.

The Difference Between Hustle and Stewardship

Let me show you the contrast:

HUSTLE asks: *"How much can I get?"*
STEWARDSHIP asks: *"How much can I sustain while staying whole?"*

HUSTLE says: *"I need to do more, be everywhere, say yes to every opportunity."*
STEWARDSHIP says: *"I will do what I'm called to do with excellence, and I will protect my peace while doing it."*

HUSTLE measures success by: *Revenue at any cost*
STEWARDSHIP measures success by: *Sustainable impact and legacy*

HUSTLE builds for: *The next quarter*
STEWARDSHIP builds for: *The next decade*

HUSTLE sacrifices: *Your body, your Sabbath, your peace*
STEWARDSHIP protects: *Your temple, your rest, your sovereignty*

We are building for longevity. We are designing for the woman who will be leading at 70 and 80 with the same grace and élan she has today—not the woman who burned out at 50 because she hustled herself into the ground.

This is what the Proverbs 31 woman modeled. She was a strategic entrepreneur who built multiple revenue streams. But she wasn't exhausted. She wasn't depleted. She was clothed in strength and dignity, and she could laugh at the future.

That's what we're building.

Your Sabbath-Compatible Business Model

A Kingdom business must be able to breathe. It must be able to survive the Sabbath.

If your business model requires you to work seven days a week to succeed, it's not a Kingdom business. It's a hustle dressed up in faith language.

To build a business that honors rest and sovereignty, we design revenue streams that work even when we're not working. Not because we're lazy, but because we're wise.

This is the model I use and teach:

1. Private Advisory (The High-Touch)
What it is: This is for the woman who needs a Chief Legacy Architect in her corner. She's navigating reinvention, building a Kingdom business, or transitioning from depletion to embodied sovereignty. She needs strategic guidance, embodiment coaching, and protective wisdom.

Structure:
- 3-5 clients maximum at any time
- 3-6 month engagements
- On YOUR schedule (Monday-Thursday, no weekends)
- Deep, transformational work

Investment: $7k-$15k per engagement

Why it works for the Sovereign Soft Life:
- High-touch, high-value work that doesn't require volume
- Scheduled calls protect your Sabbath
- You work with women who respect your boundaries
- Deep impact without depletion

Annual potential: $40k-$75k (with 3-5 clients per year)

2. Short-Term Cohorts (The Collective)

What it is: "The Sovereign Soft Life" group experience. Women gather for 6-8 weeks to learn embodiment, Sabbath-honoring business, and how to remove unnecessary weight.

Structure:
- 6-8 week programs
- 2-3 cohorts per year
- Weekly live calls (scheduled, not emergency-responsive)
- Community support between calls

Investment: $997-$1,997 per person

Why it works for the Sovereign Soft Life:

- Scheduled cohorts mean you know exactly when you're working

- Group work allows you to serve more women without one-on-one depletion

- Live calls can be recorded and reused as digital products later

- Clear start and end dates protect your rest between cohorts

Annual potential: $20k-$60k (with 10-30 women per year)

3. Quarterly Masterclasses (The Deep Dive)
What it is: 90-minute intensive workshops on specific embodiment topics:

- "Embodied Faith: Your Body as Temple"
- "The Proverbs 31 Blueprint for Modern Women"
- "Building the Sovereign Soft Life"

Structure:

- One Saturday per quarter (but NOT on your Sabbath—schedule for early evening after your Sabbath ends)

- Live teaching + Q&A

- Recorded and available as replay

Investment: $97-$197 per person

Why it works for the Sovereign Soft Life:
- Four times a year is sustainable
- Recorded sessions become evergreen products
- Short, focused teaching doesn't deplete you
- Can be done from anywhere with internet

Annual potential: $10k-$20k (with 20-30 people per masterclass)

4. Speaking & Teaching (The Authority)
What it is: Sharing the message at conferences, churches, women's events, and faith-based business gatherings.

Topics:
- Embodiment and the Sovereign Soft Life
- The Proverbs 31 Woman Reimagined

- From Survival to Sovereignty
- Sabbath-Honoring Business Building

Structure:
- Booked in advance (no last-minute requests)
- Travel requirements negotiated to protect your energy
- Speaking fee + expenses

Investment: $2k-$7k per engagement

Why it works for the Sovereign Soft Life:
- You control how many engagements you accept
- Speaking establishes authority and leads to other revenue streams
- Can be scheduled around your Sabbath and rest needs

Annual potential: $10k-$35k (with 5-10 engagements per year)

5. Digital Products (The Evergreen)
What it is: Ebooks, guides, workbooks, and courses that sell while you sleep.

Examples:

- *"Becoming Her: The Sovereign Soft Life of a Kingdom Woman"*

- "Healing Whispers" companion resources

- "The Embodiment Toolkit"

- "Sabbath Business Planning Guide"

Structure:

- Created once, sold forever

- Automated sales funnels

- No live delivery required

Investment: $27-$497

Why it works for the Sovereign Soft Life:
- TRUE passive income
- Works while you're observing Sabbath
- Scales without consuming more of your time
- Serves women who aren't ready for high-ticket yet

Annual potential: $5k-$20k (and grows over time)

6. High-Level Retreats (The Immersive)
What it is: 2-3 times per year, 10-20 women gather for 2-3 days to experience what embodied, sovereign soft life feels like.

Structure:
- Curated locations (Vegas, desert retreats, mountain sanctuaries)
- Deep embodiment work
- Sabbath practice
- Community and connection

Investment: $2k-$5k per attendee

Why it works for the Sovereign Soft Life:
- Only 2-3 times per year (sustainable)
- High-value, high-impact experience
- Retreats can be scheduled around your rest needs
- Creates deep relationships with ideal clients

Annual potential: $40k-$100k (with 20-30 women total across all retreats)

Your Total Annual Potential

Year 1 (Building Phase): $75k-$150k
Year 2-3 (Established): $150k-$300k+

And here's what's crucial: You're not working 60-hour weeks to hit these numbers.

You're working 20-30 focused hours per week, Monday-Thursday. Your Sabbath is protected. Your peace is intact. Your body is a temple, not a tool.

This is what stewardship looks like.

The Tech & Automation: Your Sacred Digital Architecture

The "*Laptop Lifestyle*" is often sold as working from a beach in a bikini. But for the Sovereign woman, it means something different: location independence and time freedom.

It means you can build from anywhere—your Vegas sanctuary, your son's house, a quiet cabin in the mountains—and your business still runs.

We utilize automation—email sequences, sales funnels, scheduling systems, payment processors—to ensure the business runs while we rest.

This isn't about being "lazy." This is about being a wise steward of your energy.

By automating the "Precision" (the P in P.R.I.V.É.), you free up your soul for the "Visionary" work.

What to Automate

Email sequences: Welcome new subscribers, nurture leads, deliver digital products

Scheduling systems: Let clients book calls during your available hours only

Payment processing: Accept payments 24/7 without manual invoicing

Course delivery: Automatically grant access to digital products after purchase

Social media: Schedule posts in advance (but still show up live when it matters)

When your digital products are selling on autopilot, you aren't tied to a desk. You can be in Las Vegas with your family for Thanksgiving, or taking a Sabbath walk in the desert, knowing that your "Sacred Architecture" is holding the line.

This is freedom. This is sovereignty.

The Financial Vision: Building for Legacy

Let's be clear about what we're building for.

Not just revenue. Legacy.

Not just survival. Sovereignty.

Not just getting through this year. Building for the woman you'll be at 70 and 80.

Year 1: The Foundation Year ($75k-$150k)

This is the year you prove the concept.

You're not trying to scale yet. You're establishing your authority, refining your message, and building systems that protect your Sabbath.

What Year 1 looks like:
- Launch one signature digital product (an ebook, a guide, a course)
- Run your first cohort or masterclass to test your teaching
- Take on 2-3 private advisory clients who align with your values
- Build your email list through consistent, valuable content
- Establish your systems and automation so the business can breathe

This year is about foundation, not frenzy. You're learning what works, gathering testimonials, and building a sustainable rhythm. You're protecting your Sabbath while you build.

Year 2-3: The Leverage Year ($150k-$300k+)
This is the year you scale through systems, not through exhaustion.

You're not working more hours—you're working with more leverage. Your digital products do the heavy lifting. Your reputation attracts ideal clients. Your boundaries are respected.

What Year 2-3 looks like:
- Evergreen products generating passive income while you rest
- 3-5 consistent advisory clients who value your wisdom
- 2-3 cohorts per year with waitlists
- Speaking engagements that establish your authority
- 1-2 high-level retreats that create deep transformation
- Systems running so smoothly you can take a two-week vacation without everything falling apart

And your Sabbath? Still protected. Your peace? Still intact. Your body? Still a temple.

This is sustainable Kingdom business. This is what it looks like to build from stewardship, not hustle.

The Application: Your Business Architecture

THE APPLICATION: Choose Your Entry Point
You don't have to do all of these exercises right now. Choose the one that will move you forward today.

If you're feeling depleted by your current work: Start with Business Embodiment Check

If your business is violating your rest: Start with Sabbath Business Audit

If you're ready to design your revenue model: Start with Revenue Model Design

If you're ready to launch something: Start with Map Your First Offering

1. Business Embodiment Check
Be brutally honest: Is your current work serving your life or consuming it?

Answer these questions:

- If you disappeared for two weeks, would your business collapse?
- Do you feel energized after a work day, or depleted?
- Can you take a full Sabbath without checking email?
- Are you building for legacy, or just surviving quarter to quarter?
- Does your business honor your body as a temple, or treat it like a tool?

Where is the "unnecessary friction" in your revenue model?

Maybe it's:
- A service that requires constant availability
- A client who doesn't respect boundaries
- A manual process that's eating your time
- A pricing structure that requires volume to survive

Identify one point of friction. Commit to removing it in the next 30 days.

2. Sabbath Business Audit
What is one thing you are doing in your business that requires you to violate your rest?

Is it:
- A client who expects weekend responses?
- A service that demands emergency availability?
- A social media strategy that has you posting seven days a week?
- A manual process you do on Saturdays "to catch up"?

Commit to changing this one thing in the next 30 days.

Maybe that means:
- Having a conversation with a client about boundaries
- Automating a process
- Removing a service from your offerings
- Hiring someone to handle weekend inquiries

Your Sabbath is non-negotiable. Your business must bend to honor it, not the other way around.

3. Revenue Model Design

Looking at the six revenue streams above, which two feel most aligned with your current energy?

Hint: Start with one "Evergreen" (like a digital product) and one "High-Touch" (like advisory or a cohort).

For each one, answer:

- Who is this for?

- What transformation does it deliver?

- How does it protect my Sabbath?

- What's the investment level that feels like "strength and dignity" (Proverbs 31:25)?

You don't need all six streams. You need the two that allow you to serve powerfully while staying sovereign.

4. Map Your First Offering

If you were to launch your first "Sovereign" offer in the next 60-90 days, what would it be?

Answer these questions:

Who is it for?

- Be specific. Not "women." Which women? Women in what season? Women facing what challenge?

What transformation does it deliver?

- What's the before and after? What changes for them?

How does it protect your peace while delivering their transformation?

- Is it a cohort with set boundaries? A digital product? Scheduled advisory calls?

What is the price point that feels like "Strength and Dignity" (Proverbs 31:25)?

- Not "what will people pay?" What does YOUR sovereignty require?

Write this down. This is your blueprint.

The Truth About Kingdom Business

You don't have to choose between impact and income. You don't have to sacrifice your body to build wealth. You don't have to violate your Sabbath to scale.

You can build a business that serves your life, honors your temple, protects your rest, and creates sustainable legacy.

But it requires you to think differently. To move from hustle to stewardship. To design intentionally instead of reacting constantly.

The Proverbs 31 woman wasn't exhausted. She was embodied.
She wasn't depleted. She was building from overflow.
She wasn't hustling. She was stewarding.

And so can you.

Your business is not your life. Your business serves your life.

And when you build it that way—from a foundation of Sabbath rest, embodied strength, and sovereign boundaries—you create something that doesn't just generate revenue.

You create something that lasts.

In the next chapter, we'll walk through the practical 90-day roadmap for launching your first sovereign offering. Because knowing what to build is one thing. Actually building it—while navigating the messy middle of doubt, fear, and uncertainty—is another.

The foundation is set. The model is clear. Now it's time to move.

You are not too late. You are exactly on time.

REMEMBER THIS

- Hustle is rooted in fear; stewardship is rooted in faith.
- My business serves my life—it doesn't consume it.
- I build for legacy (10-20 years), not just survival (next quarter).
- Sabbath-compatible = sustainable and profitable.
- I don't need 60-hour weeks—I need 20-30 focused, intentional hours.
- I am building a business that funds my legacy without stealing my peace.

PART IV:
THE 90-DAY EMERGENCE
(The Path Forward)

I've been in a cocoon for sixteen years—wrapped in caregiving, grief, and survival.

But now, at 57, standing in my Las Vegas sanctuary with the desert sky stretched impossibly wide above me, I'm learning something I've never known: what it actually means to be *soft*.

Not soft because someone else is carrying my weight.

Soft because I've finally put down the weight that was never mine to carry.

Not soft because I'm being taken care of.

Soft because I've learned to take care of myself without depletion.

Not soft because life suddenly got easy.

Soft because I've built a life that doesn't require hardness to survive.

This is Part III: the frameworks that make sovereignty sustainable.

Here, you'll discover what the Sovereign Soft Life actually looks like in practice—how to remove unnecessary weight, how to build Sabbath as the foundation of your week (not an afterthought), and how to create Kingdom businesses that serve your life instead of consuming it.

This isn't theory. This is architecture.

These are the blueprints I'm using to build a life worth protecting—a life where my body is a temple, rest is holy, and my business funds my legacy without stealing my peace.

The cocoon is breaking open. You've learned *who* you're becoming (Part I) and *how* to embody her (Part II).

Now it's time to build the framework that makes sovereignty sustainable.

Welcome to the Sovereign Soft Life.

Chapter 11:
THE 90-DAY METAMORPHOSIS

"Being confident of this, that he who began a good work in you will carry it on to completion until the day of Christ Jesus."

- Philippians 1:6

WRITING FROM INSIDE THE COCOON

As I write this, it is January 12, 2026.

I am sitting in my Las Vegas sanctuary, looking out at the desert sky that convinced me I was home just over a year ago. My coffee is going cold because I keep stopping to stare at the blinking cursor on my screen, wondering if I have any right to be writing a book about embodiment when some mornings I still wake up and forget—just for a moment—that I'm not in Savannah anymore.

The manuscript for *Becoming Her* sits at 60,000 words. The website updates are half-done. The LinkedIn manifesto is written but not yet posted because every time I read it, a voice whispers: *"Who are you to declare sovereignty at 57?"*

This is the truth of the messy middle: I am teaching you how to become while I am still becoming.

I am not writing this book from the mountaintop. I am writing it from the trail—breathless, uncertain, committed, and absolutely convinced that if I wait until I "arrive," I will never write a word.

THE REALITY OF JANUARY 2026

Let me tell you what my 90-day emergence actually looks like right now, because the polished version won't help you when you're in your own dissolve.

This morning, I woke up at 6:00 AM without an alarm—my body's new rhythm since moving to Vegas. I did my embodied morning practice: feet on the floor, five breaths, presence before productivity. I felt strong. Sovereign. Clear.

By 10:00 AM, I was spiraling.

I had opened my email to find a message from a woman asking about private advisory. She wanted to know my credentials, my track record, my "proven results." And for a moment—just a moment—I felt like a fraud.

Who am I to charge $10,000 for advisory when I haven't even launched my first cohort yet? Who am I to teach embodiment when I'm still learning to walk without a limp after losing my toe? Who am I to talk about the Sovereign Soft Life when I'm still figuring out what "soft" even means?

I closed my laptop. I walked outside into the desert air. I placed my hand on my heart and said out loud: "You survived sepsis three times. You chose yourself at 57. You are rebuilding in real time. That IS the credential."

And then I came back inside and responded to her email.

This is metamorphosis. It's not a smooth ascent. It's a daily choice to keep inhabiting the becoming even when the old identity screams that you're not ready.

THE COCOON IS TIGHTEST RIGHT BEFORE IT BREAKS

The truth about transformation that nobody tells you: the hardest part isn't the first step. It's the middle—when you've left the old life but haven't fully stepped into the new one.

I am no longer "Survival Karen." I made the Sacred Exit. I crossed into my sovereign territory. I have done the internal work of embodiment, of releasing the weight, of setting boundaries.

But I am not yet "Established Karen" either. I don't have a full client roster. I don't have a proven business model. I haven't delivered my first cohort or hosted my first retreat.

I am in the in-between.

And the in-between is where the caterpillar dissolves into liquid before it reorganizes into a butterfly.

Inside the cocoon, there is no shape. There is no form. There is only the terrifying trust that what's happening in the dark will eventually become wings.

Some days, I feel the wings forming. I write a chapter of this book and think, *"Yes. This is it. This is what I'm here to do."* I have a conversation with a woman who says, *"Your story gave me permission to choose myself,"* and I know—absolutely know—that this work matters.

Other days, I feel like liquid. Formless. Undefined. I look at my bank account and wonder if I should just get a "real job." I scroll LinkedIn and see women with MBAs and corporate credentials and think, *"What do I have? A story of survival? A framework from a hospitality business I closed?"*

Both realities are true. And both are part of the same becoming.

THE MANIFESTO I HAVEN'T POSTED YET

The LinkedIn manifesto sits in my drafts folder. I've rewritten it twelve times.

It starts like this:

"At 57, I'm finally choosing myself. For sixteen years, I was 'Postponed Karen'—the caregiver, the widow, the survivor. I spent my life holding the center for everyone else while my own dreams waited in the wings. Then, on August 27, 2024, I made the hardest decision of my life: I chose me."

It goes on to describe the Sacred Exit, the move to Vegas, the three bouts with sepsis, the amputation, the embodiment work, the Sovereign Soft Life.

It ends with this:

"I don't know exactly who I'm becoming. But I know I'm done postponing myself. I'm done treating my body as a tool. I'm done building businesses that consume me. I'm building the Sovereign Soft Life—and I'm inviting you to build it with me."

Every time I read it, I cry. Not sad tears. Terrified tears. Grateful tears. Tears that say, *"If I post this, there's no going back."*

Because once you declare your becoming publicly, you can't hide in the cocoon anymore.

So why haven't I posted it yet?

Because I'm afraid.

I'm afraid people will think I'm too old to be starting over. I'm afraid people will judge me for leaving my mother in skilled nursing. I'm afraid people will ask why I didn't "make it work" in hospitality. I'm afraid people will see my scars—literal and metaphorical—and decide I'm not qualified to teach sovereignty.

But here's what I know: Fear is not a reason to stay silent. Fear is proof that what you're about to do matters.

So by the time you read this book, the manifesto will be posted. Not because I stopped being afraid. But because I chose to be sovereign anyway.

THE BOOK I'M WRITING WHILE LIVING IT

This book—the one you're holding—is my first product. My first proof of concept. My first public declaration that I am no longer just a survivor; I am a guide.

But I'm writing it in real time.

I am not writing from a place of "I've arrived." I am writing from a place of "I'm emerging, and I'm bringing you with me."

Every chapter is a battle. Not with the words, but with the doubt.

When I wrote Chapter 2 about the three deaths and the mandate for life, I had to stop three times because the grief came back. I sat at my desk and sobbed for the woman I was—for the James I lost, for the body that broke, for the years I spent postponing myself.

When I wrote Chapter 4 about the body as sanctuary, I had to stop and do a gratitude scan on my own body because I realized I was still, even now, treating it as optional. I was skipping meals to finish the manuscript. I was staying up late to write "just one more chapter." I was performing the very depletion I'm teaching women to release.

Embodiment isn't a destination. It's a daily practice of catching yourself mid-performance and choosing presence instead.

When I wrote Chapter 9 about Sabbath as architecture, I had to confront the fact that I had worked through the last two Sabbaths to meet my self-imposed deadline for this book. I had violated the very boundary I'm teaching as non-negotiable.

So I stopped. I closed my laptop on Friday at sundown. I rested. And on Sunday evening, when I opened the manuscript again, the words flowed.

This is the truth of the messy middle: You will teach what you're still learning. You will stumble. You will catch yourself. You will choose again.

And that—*that*—is embodiment.

WHAT THE 90 DAYS ACTUALLY FEEL LIKE

I am in Week 2 of my 90-day emergence as I write this.

Week 1 felt like freedom. I updated my website. I wrote my manifesto. I outlined this book. I felt unstoppable. I told myself, *"This is it. I'm doing it. I'm becoming."*

Week 2 feels like doubt.

The website updates are taking longer than I thought. The manifesto is still in drafts. The book is half-written, and I'm terrified no one will buy it. I've had three free "Embodiment Clarity Calls" scheduled, and two people canceled at the last minute.

I am in the wobble.

And the wobble is where most women quit.

Because the wobble doesn't feel like becoming. It feels like failing.

But here's what I'm learning: The wobble is *part* of the becoming.

The caterpillar doesn't dissolve into liquid and then immediately sprout wings. There's a stage where it's just... liquid. Formless. Uncertain. Trusting the process even though there's no visible proof that anything is happening.

That's where I am.

And if you're reading this, that might be where you are too.

So let me tell you what I tell myself every morning when the doubt shows up:

You are not failing. You are dissolving so God can remake you. Trust the process. Stay in the cocoon. The wings are forming even when you can't see them.

THE WOMEN WHO ARE WATCHING

Here's what keeps me going when I want to quit:

I think about the women who are watching.

The 52-year-old widow who sent me a DM on Instagram saying, *"Your story made me cry. I thought I was too old to start over."*

The 47-year-old caregiver who emailed me after reading one of my essays: *"I've been waiting for permission to choose myself. Thank you for giving it to me."*

The 63-year-old entrepreneur who called me and said, *"I've been hustling for 30 years. I didn't know there was another way."*

These women are not waiting for me to be perfect. They're waiting for me to be *real*.

They don't need me to have it all figured out. They need me to show them that you can choose yourself at 57. That you can rebuild after loss. That you can create the Sovereign Soft Life even when you don't know exactly what it looks like yet.

They need me to document the dissolve so they know they're not alone in theirs.

So I keep writing. I keep showing up. I keep choosing embodiment even when it's messy.

Because if I wait until I'm "ready," I will never start.

And if I never start, those women will keep waiting for someone to give them permission.

THE BREAKTHROUGH MOMENTS

It's not all wobble and doubt. There are breakthrough moments too.

Last week, I was walking in the desert—no phone, no agenda, just me and the sky—and I felt it. The shift. The undeniable knowing that I am exactly where I'm supposed to be.

I looked at the mountains in the distance and thought, *"A year ago, I was in Savannah, drowning in caregiving. Now I'm in Vegas, building a life that honors my temple. That's not failure. That's a miracle."*

Yesterday, I finished Chapter 10 on Kingdom Business, and when I read it back, I didn't recognize my own voice. It was stronger. Clearer. More authoritative. I thought, *"This is what sovereignty sounds like."*

This morning, I received a text from Benjamin: *"Mom, I'm proud of you."*

Four words. But they landed like a benediction.

Because choosing myself didn't destroy my family. It *saved* us. By choosing myself, I made space for us to finally be together—not as caregiver and dependent, but as whole people building our lives in parallel.

These breakthrough moments don't erase the wobble. But they remind me that the wobble is worth it.

THE COMMITMENT I'M MAKING

I don't know if this book will sell 20 copies or 2,000.

I don't know if my first cohort will have 6 women or 60.

I don't know if I'll hit my revenue goals for Q1 or if I'll have to recalibrate everything in April.

But here's what I do know:

I am committed to the becoming, not just the destination.

I am committed to showing up—imperfect, uncertain, sovereign—every single day.

I am committed to documenting this emergence so other women know they're not alone.

I am committed to building the Sovereign Soft Life even when I don't fully know what it looks like.

I am committed to treating my body as a temple, honoring my Sabbath, and building a business that serves my life.

And I am committed to meeting the woman I'm becoming—even though I don't fully know her yet.

This is my 90-day metamorphosis.

This is my messy middle.

This is my emergence.

And I'm inviting you to emerge with me.

THE ROADMAP: YOUR 90-DAY SACRED ARCHITECTURE

The Sovereign Soft Life is not built through hustle. It's architected through intentional, Kingdom-aligned steps. Here is the blueprint for the first 90 days—not as a rigid formula, but as a flexible framework that honors both your becoming and your rest.

MONTH 1: THE FOUNDATION (JANUARY)
Theme: Digital Sanctification & Public Declaration

The first month is about establishing your authority platform and making your becoming public. This is when you step out of the cocoon—not fully formed, but visible. This is when you say, "I am no longer hiding."

Week 1-2: Digital Sanctification
This is not about perfection. This is about presence.

Your website is your "authority home"—the digital space where women come to understand who you are and what you stand for. It doesn't need to be elaborate. It needs to be *true*.

What you're actually doing:
- Updating karenymoore.com with your embodiment story
- Creating a "Work With Me" page that reflects your sovereign offerings
- Writing your "About" page from embodied truth, not resume credentials
- Adding testimonials if you have them (and if you don't, that's okay—you're building proof of concept)

What this will feel like: You will rewrite your bio seventeen times. You will doubt every word. You will compare yourself to women with professional headshots and perfectly designed sites.

Here's what I want you to remember: Your website is not a competition. It's a declaration. It's you saying, "This is who I am. This is what I offer. If this resonates, you're my people."

The resistance that will come up:
- "My site isn't professional enough."
- "I don't have enough testimonials."
- "I need better photos."
- "I should wait until I have more to show."

How to navigate it: Done is better than perfect. Published is better than polished. Your story—raw and real—is more powerful than any stock photo or corporate bio.

Post it. Even if it's imperfect. You can always refine it later.

Week 3-4: The Public Declaration (Your Manifesto)
This is the scariest part of Month 1. This is when you go public.

Your manifesto is not a sales pitch. It's a sacred declaration. It's you telling the world: "I was postponed. I am emerging. And I'm inviting you to emerge with me."

Where to post it: LinkedIn is the platform for this work. It's where professional women gather, where thought leaders are born, where your story will resonate with the women who need to hear it.

What to include in your manifesto:
- Where you were (the cocoon, the survival, the postponed life)
- The moment everything changed (your Sacred Exit)
- Where you are now (in the messy middle, building the Sovereign Soft Life)
- The invitation (if my story resonates, come build this with me)

Example structure:
"At 57, I'm finally choosing myself.

For sixteen years, I was 'Postponed Karen'—the caregiver, the widow, the survivor. I spent my life holding the center for everyone else while my own dreams waited in the wings.

Then, on August 27, 2024, I made the hardest decision of my life: I chose me.

I left Savannah. I crossed into Las Vegas. I started rebuilding—not from what made sense, but from what felt true.

I don't know exactly who I'm becoming. But I know I'm done postponing myself. I'm done treating my body as a tool. I'm done building businesses that consume me.

I'm building the Sovereign Soft Life—a Kingdom-aligned existence where my body is a temple, rest is holy, and my business serves my life instead of consuming it.

If you're a woman in your second act (40s, 50s, 60s, 70s+) who's been postponing herself, this is your permission slip. You are not too late. You are exactly on time.

I'm documenting my emergence so you know you're not alone in yours. Come build this with me."

What this will feel like: Terrifying. Vulnerable. Like standing naked in a public square.

You will hover over the "Post" button for ten minutes. You will second-guess every word. You will wonder if anyone will care.

Post it anyway.

What will happen after you post: Some people will ignore it. Some people will scroll past. But the *right* people—the women who need to hear this—will respond. They will message you. They will thank you. They will say, "I thought I was the only one."

Those women are your people. They are the beginning of your email list, your future clients, your co-conspirators in becoming.

Week 3-4: Begin Building Your Temple Registry (Email List)

While your manifesto is circulating, you start building your "Temple Registry"—your email list.

This is not about collecting names. This is about gathering the women who are ready to become.

How to start:

- Add an email signup form to your website: "Join the Becoming Her Collective—weekly letters on embodiment, sovereignty, and the Sovereign Soft Life"

- Offer a simple lead magnet: "The 7-Day Embodiment Starter Practice" (you'll find this in the Bonus Section of this book)

- Post 3x per week on LinkedIn/Instagram with substance, not fluff
    - Monday: Faith/Scripture on embodiment and rest
    - Wednesday: Lessons from your survival/reinvention journey
    - Friday: Business wisdom (Sabbath-honoring, sovereign soft life business building)

What to post: Not motivational quotes. Not stock images. *Your story.* In bite-sized pieces.

A Monday post might be: *"1 Corinthians 6:19 says your body is a temple. But for sixteen years, I treated mine like a warehouse for everyone else's needs. Embodiment is the daily practice of treating your body with the reverence it deserves. Today, I'm practicing presence over productivity. What's one way you're honoring your temple today?"*

A Wednesday post might be: *"I survived sepsis three times. Each time, my body forced me to rest because I refused to choose it willingly. If your body is breaking down, it's not failing you—it's screaming for your attention. What is your body trying to tell you?"*

A Friday post might be: *"The Proverbs 31 woman wasn't exhausted. She was embodied. She built businesses that served her life. She laughed at the future because she was prepared, not because life was easy. You don't have to hustle yourself into the ground to build a Kingdom business. You can build from rest."*

Week 3-4: Offer 5 Free Embodiment Clarity Calls
This is how you start understanding the hearts of the women you serve.

A "Clarity Call" is not a sales call. It's a listening session. You're not pitching. You're *receiving*.

How to structure it:

- 30 minutes, Zoom or phone
- No agenda except to listen
- Ask: "Where are you in your journey? What's weighing you down? What does 'sovereign soft life' mean to you?"
- Take notes. These women are showing you what they need.

Why this matters: These calls will teach you more about your future offerings than any market research. You'll hear the exact language your people use. You'll understand their pain points. You'll know what to build.

And some of these women will become your first clients.

By the End of Month 1:
- Your website is live (imperfect but true)
- Your manifesto is posted (terrifying but necessary)
- Your email list has begun (even if it's just 10 women)
- You've had 5 clarity calls (and you understand your people)
- You're posting 3x per week (building visibility and trust)

You have laid the foundation. Now it's time to build your first offering.

MONTH 2: THE OFFERING (FEBRUARY)
Theme: Your First Digital Product & Proof of Concept

This is the month you stop *talking* about sovereignty and start *selling* it.

Your first product is not a masterpiece. It's a *milestone*. It's proof that you can create something valuable and people will exchange money for it.

For me, that first product is this book: *"Becoming Her: The Sovereign Soft Life of a Kingdom Woman."*

For you, it might be an ebook, a guide, a mini-course, or a workbook. Whatever it is, it must be:

- Rooted in your lived experience
- Solving a specific problem
- Priced accessibly (so women can say yes without overthinking)
- Delivered digitally (so it can sell while you rest)

Week 1-2: Create Your First Digital Product
Option 1: An Ebook

- 15,000-30,000 words
- Based on your story and frameworks
- Designed as a PDF (Canva templates work beautifully)
- Price: $27-$47

Option 2: A Guide or Workbook

- "The Sabbath Business Planning Guide"
- "The 30-Day Embodiment Practice"
- "The Sovereign Soft Life Blueprint"
- Price: $17-$37

Option 3: A Mini-Course (3-5 video lessons)

- "Embodied Faith: Your Body as Temple" (5 short videos + workbook)
- "Building the Sovereign Soft Life" (4 modules)

- Price: $97-$197

What this will feel like: You will doubt every word. You will compare yourself to "real" authors or course creators. You will wonder if anyone will buy it.

Create it anyway.

The resistance that will come up:
- "It's not good enough."
- "I'm not an expert."
- "People can get this information for free online."
- "What if no one buys it?"

How to navigate it: Your story is your credential. Your lived transformation is your authority. And the women who need this *cannot* get it anywhere else—because no one else has *your* story.

Price it from "Strength and Dignity" (Proverbs 31:25), not from scarcity. If it feels too low, you're undervaluing your wisdom. If it feels too high, you're pricing from fear of rejection.

Find the price that feels sovereign.

Week 2-3: Set Up Your Sales Infrastructure

You need three things:

1. **A sales page** (on your website)
2. **A payment processor** (Stripe, PayPal, or a platform like Gumroad/Stan Store)
3. **An automated delivery system** (email automation that sends the product immediately after purchase)

This sounds technical, but it's simpler than you think. Platforms like Gumroad, Stan Store, or Teachable handle all of this in one place.

What your sales page needs:

- The transformation: "This ebook will help you move from depletion to the Sovereign Soft Life"

- Who it's for: "Women in their second act who are ready to stop postponing themselves"

- What's inside: Table of contents or module breakdown

- Testimonials (if you have them—if not, that's okay)

- The price

- A "Buy Now" button

What this will feel like: Like you're selling something. Which you are. And that's okay.

You're not manipulating anyone. You're offering a solution to a real problem. You're inviting women to invest in their own becoming.

If they say yes, it's because they're ready. If they say no, it's because they're not. Neither is a reflection of your worth.

Week 3-4: Launch Your Product
This is not a $10K launch strategy. This is a quiet, sovereign release.

How to launch:

1. **Announce it on your email list first** (your people get first access)

2. **Post about it on LinkedIn/Instagram** (share the story of why you created it)

3. **Offer a pre-order discount** (15% off for the first week)

4. **Share it 3-5 times over the course of the week** (not spam—genuine invitations)

Example announcement post:
"I've spent the last 8 weeks writing something I never thought I'd write: a book.

'Becoming Her: The Sovereign Soft Life of a Kingdom Woman' is my story—the sixteen years of caregiving, the three deaths, the Sacred Exit, the move to Vegas, and the emergence I'm living right now.

But it's also YOUR roadmap. If you're a woman who's been postponing herself, this book is your permission slip to finally choose yourself.

It's messy. It's vulnerable. It's real. And it's available now for $27 (pre-order price—goes up to $37 next week).

Link in comments. Come become with me."

What will happen: Some people will buy immediately. Some will wait. Some will never buy.

Your goal is not 1,000 sales. Your goal is 20-30 women who say yes.

Because 20-30 women at $37 = $740-$1,110. That's proof of concept. That's revenue. That's validation that your work matters.

Week 4: Plan Your March Offering (While Honoring Sabbath)

While your ebook is selling on autopilot, you begin planning your first live experience for March.

You have two options:

Option 1: A 6-8 Week Cohort
- "The Sovereign Soft Life Cohort"
- 6-10 women, deep-dive transformational work
- Weekly 90-minute group calls (Monday-Thursday, not weekends)
- Voxer or community support between calls
- Price: $997-$1,997
- Revenue potential: $5,982-$19,970

Option 2: A 90-Minute Masterclass
- "Embodied Faith: Your Body as Temple"
- OR "The Proverbs 31 Blueprint for Modern Women"
- Live teaching + Q&A
- Recorded and available as replay
- Price: $97-$197
- Goal: 20-30 participants
- Revenue potential: $1,940-$5,910

Which should you choose?

If you want deep transformation and fewer women, choose the cohort. If you want broader reach and more practice teaching, choose the masterclass.

Both are valid. Both are Sabbath-compatible. Both will give you proof of concept.

What this will feel like: Exciting and terrifying in equal measure.

You'll think, "Who's going to sign up for this?" And then someone will. And then someone else. And you'll realize: They're not signing up because you're perfect. They're signing up because you're *real*.

By the End of Month 2:
- Your first digital product is live and selling
- You have 20-30 sales (proof that your work has value)
- Your March offering is planned and ready to launch
- You're still posting 3x per week
- Your email list is growing (even if it's just 50-100 women)

You have created something. You have generated revenue. You are no longer just becoming—you are *building*.

MONTH 3: THE ACTIVATION (MARCH)
Theme: Your First Live Experience & Gathering Proof

This is the month you step into your role as teacher, guide, and embodiment coach. This is when theory becomes transformation—not just for you, but for the women you serve.

This is the month you discover that you don't need to be "fully emerged" to lead others through their emergence.

Week 1: Launch Your First Live Offering
Whether you chose the cohort or the masterclass, this is launch week.

How to launch:

1. **Email your list**: "I'm opening enrollment for [offering]. Here's what we'll cover, here's the transformation, here's the investment. If you're ready, say yes."

2. **Post on LinkedIn/Instagram**: Share why you're offering this, what you've learned in your own becoming, and who it's for.

3. **Invite the women from your clarity calls**: "You told me you were struggling with [X]. This offering is designed specifically for that. I'd love to have you."

4. **Set a deadline**: Enrollment closes in 5-7 days. Not to create false urgency, but to honor your Sabbath planning. You need time to prepare.

What will happen: You will get nervous. You will wonder if anyone will sign up. And then someone will. And that first "yes" will feel like a miracle.

Maybe you'll get 6 women. Maybe 10. Maybe 30. Whatever the number, it's perfect. Because these women chose *you*—your story, your wisdom, your embodied truth.

Week 2-4 (Cohort) or Week 2 (Masterclass): Deliver Your First Live Experience
If you're running a cohort:

- Week 2: First group call (nerves and excitement)

- Week 3: Second group call (you're finding your rhythm)

- Week 4: Third group call (you're starting to see transformation in them)

If you're running a masterclass:

- Week 2: Deliver the 90-minute live session

- You'll be nervous. Your voice might shake. You might lose your train of thought.

- Do it anyway. The women in the room don't need perfect. They need *present*.

What this will feel like: The first time you teach live, you will doubt yourself. You'll compare yourself to polished speakers and established coaches.

But then something will happen: A woman will unmute herself and say, "Thank you. I needed to hear this." Or someone will message you after the call: "This changed everything for me."

And you'll realize: You don't need to be the most polished. You just need to be the most *real*.

Week 3-4: Gather Testimonials & Refine Your Messaging
As your cohort progresses or your masterclass concludes, you ask for feedback.

Not in a needy way. In a stewardship way.

How to ask: "This was my first [cohort/masterclass]. I'm committed to making this the best experience possible. Would you share what resonated most? What shifted for you? What would you tell a friend about this?"

Why this matters: Testimonials are not just marketing. They're sacred witnessing. They're women saying, "This work matters. It changed me."

And when you're in the wobble—when you're doubting whether any of this is worth it—you'll go back and read these words. And they'll remind you: Yes. This matters. Keep going.

Week 4: Sabbath Reflection & Q2 Planning
By the end of March, you've done something most women never do: You've proven the concept.

You launched a digital product. You delivered a live experience. You generated revenue. You gathered testimonials. You built an email list. You showed up—imperfect, uncertain, sovereign—every single week.

Now it's time to rest and reflect.

On your Sabbath at the end of March, ask yourself:
- What worked? What felt aligned?
- What didn't work? What felt depleting?
- What do I want to do more of in Q2?
- What do I want to release?
- Who is the woman I'm becoming after these 90 days?

By the End of Month 3:
- You've delivered your first live offering (cohort or masterclass)
- You have testimonials from real women whose lives you've impacted

- You have revenue (maybe $7K, maybe $20K, maybe $5K—whatever it is, it's proof)

- You have clarity on your next steps

- You've proven to yourself: I can do this. I am doing this. I am becoming.

THE 90-DAY TRANSFORMATION: WHAT ACTUALLY HAPPENED

Let me tell you the truth about these 90 days:

They will not be linear. They will not be easy. Some weeks you'll feel like you're flying. Other weeks you'll feel like you're drowning.

But at the end of 90 days, you will not be the same woman who started.

You will have:

- **A public declaration** (your manifesto is out there—you can't hide anymore)

- **A digital product** (something you created that didn't exist before)

- **Revenue** (proof that your work has value)

- **An email list** (your people, gathered and growing)

- **Live teaching experience** (you've stood in front of women and led them through transformation)

- **Testimonials** (sacred witnessing that this work matters)

- **Clarity** (you know what you're building and who you're becoming)

And most importantly, you will have **proof**—not for anyone else, but for yourself—that you are capable of building the Sovereign Soft Life.

You didn't wait until you were "ready." You started before you felt qualified. You documented the messy middle. You chose sovereignty even when it was terrifying.

And that, sister, is what embodiment looks like.

THE TEACHING: GRACE FOR THE DISSOLVE
The 90-day emergence is not a destination. It's a pilgrimage. And every pilgrimage requires grace for the journey.

Here's what Scripture teaches us about the wilderness seasons—the in-between times when you're no longer in Egypt but not yet in the Promised Land:

The Wilderness Is Not a Waste
The Israelites wandered in the desert for 40 years. Not because God forgot about them, but because they needed to die to their old identity before they could step into their new one.

They had to stop being "Enslaved Israel" before they could become "Sovereign Israel."

You are not wandering aimlessly. You are being refined.

Moses spent 40 years in the desert before God called him to lead. Jesus spent 40 days in the wilderness before He began His ministry. Even the Proverbs 31 woman didn't build her vineyard overnight—vineyards take *years* to produce fruit.

Your 90 days are not the finish line. They're the foundation.
Exodus 16:4 says, *"Then the Lord said to Moses, 'I will rain down bread from heaven for you. The people are to go out each day and gather enough for that day.'"*

God gave the Israelites manna daily. Not weekly. Not monthly. *Daily*.

Why? Because He was teaching them to trust Him one day at a time.

You don't need to have Q2, Q3, and Q4 figured out right now. You just need to show up today. You just need to do the next right thing.

The Cocoon Is Tightest Right Before It Breaks

2 Corinthians 4:8-9 says, *"We are hard pressed on every side, but not crushed; perplexed, but not in despair; persecuted, but not abandoned; struck down, but not destroyed."*

The messy middle will feel like you're being crushed. But you're not. You're being *compressed* so you can emerge stronger.

The cocoon is not comfortable. It's dark. It's tight. It's disorienting. But it's necessary.

Inside the cocoon, the caterpillar doesn't just grow wings. It *dissolves*. Its entire body breaks down into liquid. And then—through a process scientists still don't fully understand—it reorganizes into something entirely new.

You are not failing. You are liquefying.

And liquefying is part of the design.

THE STAGES OF THE 90-DAY DISSOLVE

Let me give you a roadmap for the emotional arc of these 90 days, because when you know what's coming, you can navigate it with grace instead of panic.

Week 1-2: The Honeymoon Phase ("I'm doing it!")
You feel unstoppable. You update your website, write your manifesto, start building. You think, "This is easier than I thought. I'm going to crush this."

Enjoy this phase. It won't last.

Week 3-5: The Wobble ("Who am I kidding?")
The initial excitement wears off. You start comparing yourself to others. You wonder if anyone actually cares. You check your email obsessively for sales notifications that aren't coming yet.

This is when most women quit.

How to navigate it: Remember why you started. Go back and read your manifesto. Call a friend who believes in you. Take a Sabbath walk and remind yourself: "I am not failing. I am dissolving."

Week 6-8: The Grind ("This is harder than I thought.")
You're in the middle of creating your product or preparing your live offering. The work is harder than you expected. Your body is tired. Your mind is full. You start to wonder if you should just get a "normal job."

This is the longest, darkest part of the cocoon.

How to navigate it: One step at a time. One word at a time. One day at a time.

You don't need to finish the whole book today. You just need to write one page. You don't need to have your entire business figured out. You just need to do the next right thing.

And rest. For the love of God, rest. Your Sabbath is not optional. It's the foundation that keeps you from collapsing.

Week 9-10: The Breakthrough ("Oh... this is actually working.")
You get your first sale. Or your first testimonial. Or someone messages you and says, "Your story changed my life."

And something shifts. You realize: This is real. This matters. I'm not just becoming—I'm *building*.

How to navigate it: Don't let the breakthrough make you cocky. Stay grounded. Stay humble. Stay committed to the process, not just the outcome.

Week 11-12: The Recalibration ("What do I keep? What do I release?")
By the end of 90 days, you'll have clarity. You'll know what's working and what isn't. You'll know which parts of the plan to double down on and which to let go.

This is not failure. This is wisdom.

The goal is not to do everything perfectly. The goal is to learn what works *for you*—for your body, your peace, your Sabbath, your sovereignty.

How to navigate it: Reflect without judgment. What felt aligned? What felt forced? What energized you? What depleted you?

Then design Q2 accordingly.

EMBODIMENT IS NOT A DESTINATION

Romans 12:2 says, *"Do not conform to the pattern of this world, but be transformed by the renewing of your mind."*

Transformation is not a one-time event. It's a daily practice of *renewing*.

Embodiment is the same.

You don't "arrive" at embodiment and then stay there forever. You practice it. Every day. Every time you choose presence over productivity. Every time you choose rest over hustle. Every time you choose your sanctuary over a sacrifice.

Some days you'll feel fully embodied—present, sovereign, clear.

Other days you'll feel like "Survival Karen" again—reactive, depleted, uncertain.

Both are part of the same becoming.

The goal is not to never wobble. The goal is to catch yourself mid-wobble and choose sovereignty anyway.

THE DIFFERENCE BETWEEN PRODUCTIVE DISCOMFORT AND DESTRUCTIVE DEPLETION

How do you know when to push and when to rest?

Here's the distinction:

Productive discomfort feels like stretching. It's uncomfortable, but it's growth. You're nervous, but you're not breaking. You're uncertain, but you're not drowning. You finish the day tired but *energized*.

Destructive depletion feels like tearing. It's not just uncomfortable—it's damaging. You're not growing; you're fragmenting. You're not tired; you're *empty*. Your body is screaming for rest, but you keep pushing anyway.

How to tell the difference:

Ask yourself these questions:

- Is my Sabbath being honored? (If no, you're in depletion.)
- Am I energized or drained after working? (Energized = productive. Drained = destructive.)
- Is my body giving me warning signs? (Headaches, insomnia, stomach issues, chronic tension—these are your body saying "STOP.")
- Am I building from overflow or from fumes? (Overflow = sustainable. Fumes = about to crash.)

If you're in destructive depletion, stop. Rest. Recalibrate. Your business can wait. Your body cannot.

THE SABBATH FILTER APPLIES TO THE 90 DAYS TOO

You already know the Sabbath Filter from Chapter 9. Now apply it to your 90-day emergence:

1. **Is this emergency-responsive?** If it requires you to be "on call" 24/7, it doesn't fit your architecture.

2. **Does it respect the weekend?** If it requires you to work through Sabbath, redesign it.

3. **Is it built to honor rest?** If it depletes you, it's not sustainable.

You don't have to sacrifice your Sabbath to build a business. In fact, you *can't*. Because a business built on depletion will collapse the moment you stop hustling.

The Sovereign Soft Life is only possible when Sabbath is the foundation.

GRACE FOR THE DAYS YOU FEEL LIKE LIQUID

There will be days—maybe even weeks—when you feel formless. When you look at the 90-day plan and think, "I can't do this."

On those days, I want you to remember:

The caterpillar doesn't know it's becoming a butterfly.
Inside the cocoon, it has no idea what's happening. It just knows it's dissolving. It just knows it's dark. It just knows it's uncomfortable.

But the dissolve is not destruction. It's *reorganization*.

You are not falling apart. You are being *remade*.

And the woman you're becoming? She's worth the discomfort.

Psalm 46:10 says, *"Be still, and know that I am God."*

On the days you feel like liquid, be still. Rest in the knowing that God is not done with you yet.

The wings are forming even when you can't see them.

THE APPLICATION: YOUR PERSONAL 90-DAY EMERGENCE PLAN

Now it's your turn. Let's take the roadmap and make it *yours*.

THE APPLICATION: Choose Your Entry Point

You don't have to do all of these exercises right now. Choose the one that feels most urgent.

If you're ready to map your 90 days: Start with Exercise 1: Your 90-Day Sacred Architecture

If you need weekly accountability: Start with Exercise 2: The Weekly Sovereignty Check-In

If you're in the wobble and need grace: Start with Exercise 3: Your Permission Slips

If you want to track your becoming: Start with Exercise 4: The Becoming Journal

If you need a visual roadmap: Start with Exercise 5: The Messy Middle Map

Exercise 1: Your 90-Day Sacred Architecture
Using the roadmap from this chapter, design your own 90-day emergence plan.

Month 1 (Foundation) - My Goals:
1. Digital Sanctification:
    - What needs to be updated on my website?
    - What's the ONE thing I want my "About" page to communicate?
    - When will I have this done by? (Be specific: "By January 20th")

2. My Manifesto:
    - What platform will I post it on?
    - What's the core message? (In one sentence)
    - When will I post it? (Pick a date—and commit)
3. Building My Email List:
    - What will I offer as a lead magnet?
    - How many times per week will I post? (Be realistic—3x is ideal, but even 2x is progress)
    - How many Embodiment Clarity Calls will I offer? (5 is the goal, but even 3 is valuable)

Month 2 (Offering) - My Goals:
1. My First Digital Product:
    - What will it be? (Ebook, guide, mini-course)
    - What transformation does it deliver?
    - What's my target completion date?
    - What's my price point? (Remember: "Strength and Dignity," not scarcity)
2. My Launch Plan:
    - When will I launch? (Pick a week in February)
    - How will I announce it? (Email list first, then social)
    - What's my goal? (20-30 sales is realistic and meaningful)

Month 3 (Activation) - My Goals:
1. My First Live Offering:
    - Will it be a cohort or a masterclass?
    - What will I teach?
    - When will I launch enrollment?
    - What's my target number of participants?
    - What's the price?
2. My Q2 Vision:
    - By the end of March, what do I want to have learned?
    - What do I want to have released?
    - Who do I want to be becoming?

Write this down. Print it out. Put it somewhere you'll see it every day.

This is your blueprint. Not set in stone, but set in *intention*.

Exercise 2: The Weekly Sovereignty Check-In
Every Friday before your Sabbath begins, spend 10 minutes with this reflection practice.

The Weekly Sovereignty Check-In Template:
This week, I chose sovereignty when: (Example: "I said no to a client call that would have violated my Sabbath." Or "I rested even though I wanted to keep working.")

This week, I wobbled when: (Example: "I compared myself to a woman with a bigger email list." Or "I doubted whether anyone would buy my ebook.")

This week, my body told me: (Example: "I was clenching my jaw during emails—sign I need to set better boundaries." Or "I slept without an alarm and woke up energized—sign I'm building from rest.")

This week, I'm grateful for: (Example: "A woman messaged me and said my manifesto gave her permission to choose herself." Or "I finished Chapter 3 of my ebook.")

Next week, I commit to: (Example: "Honoring my full Sabbath, no exceptions." Or "Posting 3x even if I'm scared.")

This is not about perfection. This is about presence.

You're tracking your *becoming*, not just your metrics. You're witnessing the woman you're turning into, one week at a time.

Exercise 3: Your Permission Slips
The messy middle requires permission slips—written reminders that you're allowed to be imperfect, uncertain, and sovereign all at once.

Write these out. Sign them. Date them. Come back to them when the wobble shows up.

Permission Slip #1: I give myself permission to be imperfect.
"My website doesn't have to be perfect. My manifesto doesn't have to be flawless. My first product doesn't have to be a masterpiece. I give myself permission to start before I'm ready, because 'ready' is a moving target and I will never feel fully prepared."

Signed: _____ Date: _____

Permission Slip #2: I give myself permission to wobble.

"Some days I will feel like the sovereign woman I'm becoming. Other days I will feel like 'Survival Me' again. Both are part of the same journey. I give myself permission to doubt, to question, to feel uncertain—and to choose sovereignty anyway."

Signed: _____ Date: _____

Permission Slip #3: I give myself permission to rest.

"I will not sacrifice my Sabbath for my business. I will not work through exhaustion to prove my worth. I give myself permission to rest—not as a reward, but as a requirement. My body is a temple, and rest is how I honor it."

Signed: _____ Date: _____

Permission Slip #4: I give myself permission to start small.

"I don't need 1,000 sales. I need 20. I don't need a massive email list. I need my people. I don't need to be the biggest or the loudest. I just need to be real. I give myself permission to start small and grow sustainably."

Signed: _____ Date: _____

Permission Slip #5: I give myself permission to change my mind.

"This 90-day plan is a framework, not a prison. If something isn't working, I can adjust. If something feels depleting, I can release it. I give myself permission to design my business around my sovereignty, not around what I 'should' do."

Signed: _____ Date: _____

Keep these somewhere you'll see them when the doubt shows up.

Because it will. And when it does, you'll need the reminder: You gave yourself permission to be exactly where you are.

Exercise 4: The Becoming Journal
This is not a productivity journal. This is a *witness journal*. You're documenting the emergence—not just the milestones, but the moments.

How to use it:

Every evening (or every Sabbath, if daily feels like too much), spend 5-10 minutes writing:

Week 1 Prompt: "Who am I becoming that I wasn't last week?"

Week 2 Prompt: "What did I choose this week that 'Survival Me' never would have chosen?"

Week 3 Prompt: "Where did I feel embodied this week? (Even if just for a moment.)"

Week 4 Prompt: "What permission slip do I need to write for myself this week?"

Week 5 Prompt: "What fear showed up this week? How did I respond to it?"

Week 6 Prompt: "What boundary did I hold this week that protected my peace?"

Week 7 Prompt: "What evidence do I have that this work matters? (A testimonial, a message, a sale, a feeling.)"

Week 8 Prompt: "If I could tell 'Week 1 Me' one thing, what would it be?"

Week 9 Prompt: "What breakthrough—big or small—happened this week?"

Week 10 Prompt: "What do I need to release as I move toward the end of this 90-day arc?"

Week 11 Prompt: "What have I learned about myself that I didn't know 11 weeks ago?"

Week 12 Prompt: "Who am I now? And who am I becoming next?"

This journal is sacred.

Years from now, you'll go back and read it. And you'll remember: *This is when I chose myself. This is when I became.*

Exercise 5: The Messy Middle Map
This is a visual tool for tracking both the wobbles and the wins.

How to create it:

1. Draw a horizontal line across a page. This represents your 90 days.
2. Mark Week 1 on the left, Week 12 on the right.
3. Every week, plot two points:
    - **A "Wobble Point"** (below the line): What challenged you this week? Where did you doubt?
    - **A "Win Point"** (above the line): What went well this week? What evidence of becoming did you see?

By the end of 90 days, you'll have a visual map of your emergence.

You'll see that the wobbles don't erase the wins. You'll see that even in the hardest weeks, there were breakthrough moments. You'll see that the line is never straight—but it's always moving forward.

Example:

Week 1:

- Wobble: "Scared to post my manifesto"
- Win: "Updated my website and it felt true"

Week 5:

- Wobble: "Only 3 people signed up for clarity calls (not 5)"
- Win: "Those 3 conversations were so rich—I understand my people now"

Week 9:

- Wobble: "Terrified to go live with my first masterclass"
- Win: "30 women showed up. One woman cried during Q&A and thanked me."

This map will remind you: The messy middle is not failure. It's metamorphosis.

THE TRUTH ABOUT YOUR 90 DAYS
By the end of 90 days, you will not be the same woman who started.

You won't have it all figured out. You won't be "fully emerged." You won't be a millionaire or a household name.

But you will have done something most women never do:

You will have chosen yourself. Publicly. Imperfectly. Sovereignly.

You will have built something from nothing. You will have turned your survival into wisdom and your wisdom into an offering. You will have proven—not to the world, but to *yourself*—that you are capable of becoming.

And that is everything.

Because the woman you're becoming doesn't need permission from anyone else. She just needs your commitment to keep showing up.

The cocoon is breaking open. The wings are forming. And you—imperfect, uncertain, sovereign—are ready to fly.

In the next chapter, I'll offer you the final invitation: to meet the woman you're becoming. Not someday. Not when you're "ready." But now—exactly as you are, exactly where you are.

Because you are not too late. You are exactly on time.

REMEMBER THIS

- Metamorphosis is messy—the cocoon breaks in stages, not all at once.
- The wobble is PART of becoming, not evidence of failure.
- I don't need to be "ready"—I just need to start.
- Grace for the dissolve: some days I'm liquid, and that's necessary.
- The 90 days prove the concept—my becoming continues beyond them.
- I am not too late. I am exactly on time.

CONCLUSION:
THE INVITATION TO MEET HER

"Now to him who is able to do immeasurably more than all we ask or imagine, according to his power that is at work within us."
— ***Ephesians 3:20***

The Invitation to Become (The final call to sovereignty)

Conclusion: THE INVITATION TO MEET HER

The Story: January 2026—The View from the Desert

As I write these final words, it is January 12, 2026.

Outside my window in Las Vegas, the desert stretches endlessly toward mountains that glow rose-gold in the morning light. The sky is impossibly wide—so different from the tree-lined streets of Savannah where I spent sixteen years looking down instead of up, watching for falls instead of watching for signs of my own life.

For the first time since May 5, 2009—the day James died—I am not listening for a monitor to beep. I am not bracing for the next medical crisis. I am not negotiating my peace with a world that wants to consume it.

I am simply here. Present. Embodied. Sovereign.

And I am standing in my power at 57.

Who I Am Today

I'll be honest with you: I don't know every version of the woman I am becoming yet. She is still revealing herself to me—in the quiet of my Sabbath mornings, in the moments when I catch my reflection and don't immediately look away, in the conversations with women who tell me my story gave them permission to choose themselves.

She is the woman who walks differently now. Not with a limp from the amputation, but with a different kind of stride—shoulders back, chin up, feet planted. She is the woman who says "no" without an explanation and "yes" only when it aligns with her sanctuary.

She is the woman who finally understands that her body is not a warehouse for other people's needs. It's a temple. And she treats it accordingly.

She is the woman who honors her Sabbath without guilt, who builds businesses that serve her life instead of consuming it, who protects her peace with the same fierceness she once used to hold everyone else's center.

I am still meeting her. Some days I recognize her immediately. Other days she feels like a stranger I'm learning to trust.

But here is what I know for certain:

I am fiercely committed to her. I am determined to protect her. And I am finally focused enough to let her lead.

The Woman I Was vs. The Woman I'm Becoming

Let me show you the shift:

The woman I was woke up to the sound of a walker on hardwood floors at 3 AM and didn't go back to sleep because her body had forgotten what rest felt like.

The woman I'm becoming wakes up naturally, without an alarm, and takes five breaths before she even checks her phone. She practices presence before productivity.

The woman I was believed that her value was measured by how much she could carry for others—the more weight, the more worth.

The woman I'm becoming knows that her value is inherent. She is a daughter of the King, and that is credential enough.

The woman I was treated her body like a tool—something to be used, pushed, broken if necessary, as long as everyone else was taken care of.

The woman I'm becoming treats her body like a temple—something to be honored, rested, stewarded with reverence and care.

The woman I was built businesses that required her constant presence, her perpetual availability, her endless sacrifice.

The woman I'm becoming builds businesses that work while she rests, that honor her Sabbath, that serve her life instead of consuming it.

The woman I was apologized for needing rest, for setting boundaries, for choosing herself.

The woman I'm becoming doesn't apologize for sovereignty. She simply lives it.

This transition from "Survival Karen" to "Sovereign Karen" wasn't just a relocation of my furniture from Savannah to Vegas. It was a relocation of my soul. It was learning that my fortitude—the strength that carried me through sixteen years of caregiving, three bouts with sepsis, widowhood, and loss—wasn't just for everyone else's benefit.

It was for my own emergence.

What I'm Building Now

At 57, I am building the life I never knew was possible.

I am writing this book, my first public declaration that I am no longer just a survivor but a guide.

I am preparing to launch my first cohort, my first masterclass, my first retreats where women will gather to learn what I'm still learning: how to embody sovereignty, how to build the Sovereign Soft Life, how to become the Proverbs 31 woman reimagined for modern times.

I am building an email list of women who are ready to choose themselves—not someday, but now.

I am posting on LinkedIn and Instagram, documenting my emergence in real time, showing women that you don't have to wait until you're "ready" to start becoming.

I am learning to trade and invest—not just to teach it, but for my own wealth-building, for my own legacy, for the financial sovereignty that allows me to build from overflow instead of scarcity.

And most importantly, I am finally living in the same city as my son Benjamin. After years of separation—him in the Air Force, then Denver, me in Savannah drowning in caregiving—we are building our lives in parallel again. We had our first Thanksgiving together since 2011. Our first Christmas together since 2016.

By choosing myself, I didn't lose my family. I *saved* us.

The Journey From Here

I don't know what Year 2 or Year 3 will look like. I don't know if I'll hit every revenue goal or if I'll have to recalibrate. I don't know if my first cohort will have 6 women or 60.

But I know this:

I am committed to the becoming, not just the destination.

I am committed to building the Sovereign Soft Life—for myself first, and then as a model for other women.

I am committed to honoring my Sabbath, treating my body as a temple, and protecting my peace with the same strength I once used to hold everyone else's world together.

I am committed to meeting the woman I'm becoming—even though I don't fully know her yet.

And I am inviting you to meet her too.

Because if I can choose myself at 57—after sixteen years of caregiving, three bouts with sepsis, widowhood, an amputation, and a lifetime of being "Postponed Karen"—then you can choose yourself too.

Wherever you are. Whatever your age. Whatever your story.

You are not too late. You are exactly on time.

The Teaching: This Is What Metamorphosis Looks Like

The Myth of "Too Late"
There is a cultural myth—reinforced by social media, by corporate America, by well-meaning family members—that says after a certain age, or after a certain amount of trauma, we are simply "settled" into who we are.

The myth says:

- If you didn't start your business in your 20s, you missed your window
- If you spent your 40s caregiving, your dreams are over
- If you're 50+, it's time to "slow down" and accept your limitations
- If you've been through trauma, the best you can hope for is to survive, not thrive

I am here to tell you: **That is a lie.**

Whether you are 47, 52, 57, 63, 70, or beyond—your metamorphosis is waiting for your "Yes."

Scripture is full of women who became in their second acts:

- **Sarah** gave birth to Isaac at 90—when everyone said she was "too old"

- **Naomi** rebuilt her life after loss and became the grandmother of King David's lineage—in her later years

- **Anna the prophetess** served in the temple into her 80s and was honored for her faithfulness (Luke 2:36-38)

God doesn't operate on the world's timeline. He operates on Kingdom time. And in Kingdom time, you are never too late.

You Are Not Selfish. You Are Emerging.
Let me address the lie that will try to stop you before you even start:

"Choosing yourself is selfish."

No. Choosing yourself is *stewardship*.

You are a daughter of the King. You are a temple of the Holy Spirit (1 Corinthians 6:19). If you allow your temple to be desecrated by constant depletion, boundary violations, and self-abandonment, you are not being faithful. You are being *foolish*.

Choosing yourself is not abandoning your family or your faith. It is honoring the life God gave you. It is recognizing that you cannot pour from empty. It is understanding that the greatest gift you can give to the Kingdom is a whole woman, not a hollowed-out sacrifice.

When you become a sanctuary, everyone who enters your sphere experiences the peace of God *through* you.

When you are embodied, rested, sovereign—you lead differently. You love differently. You serve differently.

Not from depletion, but from overflow.

Not from obligation, but from alignment.

Not from performance, but from presence.

This is not selfish. This is sacred.

Who Do You Become?

Let me ask you the question I've been asking myself for the last year:

Who do you become when you stop performing?

Who do you become when you're no longer "the strong one" who has to hold everyone else's world together?

Who do you become when productivity is no longer your measure of worth?

Who do you become when your body is finally treated as a temple instead of a tool?

You become a woman who laughs at the future.

Like the Proverbs 31 woman, you become someone who is prepared—not because life is easy, but because you've built a Sacred Architecture that protects your peace. You've removed unnecessary weight. You've honored Sabbath. You've created systems that allow your business to breathe. You've trained your body to be strong.

You're not afraid of what's coming because you've done the work in the present.

You become a woman who builds legacies that last.

Not legacies built on the sand of exhaustion, but legacies built on the rock of stewardship, wisdom, and Kingdom alignment.

You're not just surviving quarter to quarter. You're building for generations. You're planting vineyards that will produce fruit long after you're gone.

You become a woman who moves with élan and excellence.

Not because you're perfect, but because you're sovereign.

You do fewer things, but you do them with distinction. You speak with wisdom because you've earned it through survival and embodiment. You lead with grace because you're no longer operating from a place of depletion.

People recognize mastery when they see it. And they will see it in you.

This is what metamorphosis looks like.

Not a smooth, linear transformation. But a messy, sacred, necessary dissolve followed by a gradual reorganization into something you never imagined you could be.

The Invitation: Stop Looking Back, Start Looking Forward

For too long, you've been looking back at what was lost:

- The years you "wasted" caregiving
- The dreams you deferred
- The version of yourself you used to be before the trauma
- The body you had before illness
- The life you thought you'd have by now

But metamorphosis requires you to stop looking at the cocoon and start looking at the wings.

This is the invitation:

Stop measuring yourself by what you lost and start recognizing what you're *gaining*.

You're gaining wisdom that can only come from survival.

You're gaining authority that can only come from embodied transformation.

You're gaining the sovereignty that comes from finally choosing yourself.

You're gaining a story that will give other women permission to choose themselves too.

This is not about erasing the past. It's about honoring it—and then building something new.

The sixteen years I spent caregiving were not wasted. They were devotion. They were sacrifice. They were love in its purest form.

But that season is over.

And the season of becoming has begun.

The Final Blessing

Before I send you forward, I want to pray over you—not as a pastor, but as a fellow traveler who understands the weight you've been carrying.

My prayer for you is this:
May you feel the weight of your own dignity today. Not the weight of obligation, but the weight of *worth*. May you realize that the strength you used to survive was just a rehearsal for the strength you will use to thrive.

May your Sabbath become a sanctuary—a 24-hour perimeter around your peace where the world cannot reach you, where you remember that you are God's daughter before you are anyone's helper.

May your body become a temple—treated with reverence, honored with rest, stewarded with wisdom. May you stop apologizing for its limits and start celebrating its loyalty.

May your business become a Kingdom offering—serving your life instead of consuming it, built from overflow instead of depletion, architected around Sabbath instead of hustle.

May your life become a masterpiece of Kingdom design—not because it's perfect, but because it's *intentional*. Because every boundary you set, every weight you release, every moment you choose embodiment over performance is a brushstroke in the portrait of the woman you're becoming.

And may you finally—*finally*—give yourself permission to meet her.

She has been waiting for you to arrive.

She is strong without apology. Soft without weakness. Sovereign without arrogance.

She is clothed in strength and dignity, and she laughs at the days to come.

She is the Proverbs 31 woman reimagined for your life, your season, your becoming.

She is you. Fully healed. Fully embodied. Fully alive.

Come meet her. She's ready.

The Path Forward: Where to Go From Here

Your becoming doesn't end with the last page of this book. It begins here.

If you've read this far, you're not looking for theory. You're looking for transformation. And transformation requires action—not hustle, but intentional, sovereign steps forward.

Here's how to continue the work:

STEP 1: Start the Embodiment Practice Today

Flip to the Bonus Section at the end of this book and begin the **7-Day Embodiment Starter Practice.**

This is your first week of training for your new life. It's simple. It's doable. And it will rewire how you show up in your body.

Don't wait until you're "ready." Don't wait until Monday. Start today.

STEP 2: Join the Community

You were not designed to become in isolation. You need a sisterhood of women who are also rejecting the hustle for the Sovereign Soft Life.

Join the waitlist for "The Becoming Her Collective"—a sacred community of women walking the path of embodiment, sovereignty, and Kingdom business building.

We are launching within the next 3-6 months, and there is a seat at the table with your name on it.

This is not just another membership. This is a gathering of women who are done performing strength and ready to embody sovereignty. This is where you'll find your people.

Visit karenymoore.com and join the waitlist.

STEP 3: Take the Next Step in Your Business

If you're ready to build a Sabbath-honoring, Kingdom-aligned business but you don't know where to start, I'm creating pathways for you.

For the woman ready for high-level, private strategy:

Private Advisory is for the woman who is navigating reinvention, building a Kingdom business, or transitioning from depletion to embodied sovereignty. We will architect your Sovereign Soft Life together—your business model, your boundaries, your legacy.

Limited capacity. Applications opening soon.

For the woman ready for group transformation:

"The Sovereign Soft Life" Cohort is a 6-8 week deep-dive into embodiment, Sabbath-honoring business, and removing unnecessary weight.

Waitlist opening soon.

For the woman ready for focused teaching:

Quarterly Masterclasses on topics like:

- "Embodied Faith: Your Body as Temple"
- "The Proverbs 31 Blueprint for Modern Women"
- "Building the Sovereign Soft Life"

Details coming soon.

Visit karenymoore.com for updates on how to work together.

STEP 4: Stay Connected

This is not a one-time transaction. This is an ongoing conversation.

Visit karenymoore.com for:

- Weekly essays on embodiment, sovereignty, and the Sovereign Soft Life
- Frameworks and reflections on becoming
- Invitations to new offerings as they launch
- Updates on The Becoming Her Collective

Follow me on Instagram: @kymlifestyle **Connect on LinkedIn:** Karen Y. Moore

I post 3x per week—substance, not fluff. If you want to walk this path with me, that's where I'll be showing up.

STEP 5: Share This Book

If this book gave you permission to choose yourself, it will do the same for another woman.

Think of one woman in your life who is in the cocoon—the caregiver, the martyr, the one whose dreams are on hold. The woman who needs to hear: "You are not too late."

Send her this book. Tell her your story. Invite her into her becoming.

Because when one woman emerges, she creates a permission slip for the next.

The Final Word: You Are Exactly On Time

I don't know where you are as you read these words.

Maybe you're in your car, reading on your lunch break, wondering if you'll ever have time for your own dreams.

Maybe you're in bed at 2 AM, unable to sleep because the weight of caregiving is crushing you and you don't know how much longer you can hold the center.

Maybe you're sitting in a quiet room after everyone has gone to sleep, and you're finally asking yourself: *"When is it my turn?"*

Wherever you are, whatever your age, whatever your story—hear me:

You are not too late. You are exactly on time.

The woman you're becoming has been waiting for this moment. She's been waiting for you to finally choose her. To finally prioritize her. To finally give her permission to emerge.

She doesn't need you to be perfect. She doesn't need you to have it all figured out. She just needs your "Yes."

And once you say yes, the cocoon will start to crack. Not all at once. Not smoothly. But inevitably.

You will wobble. You will doubt. You will feel like liquid some days.

But you will also feel your wings forming.

And one day—maybe not today, maybe not this month, but one day soon—you will step out of the cocoon fully. You will stretch those wings. And you will realize:

You were never too old. You were never too broken. You were never too far behind.

You were exactly where you needed to be to become exactly who you're meant to be.

This is your metamorphosis. This is your emergence. This is your becoming.

And I'll be here, standing in the desert light of my own becoming, cheering for yours.

Come meet the woman you're becoming. She has been waiting for you.

You are not too late. You are exactly on time.

I'll see you in your becoming.

With love, honor, and sovereign grace,

Karen Y. Moore
Las Vegas, Nevada

A LETTER TO THE WOMAN STILL IN THE COCOON

Dear Sister in the Cocoon,

I know it's dark where you are. I know you can't see the wings forming yet. I know you're wondering if you'll ever emerge.

I'm writing to you from the other side—not because I've fully emerged, but because I've started. And I need you to know: the cocoon is not a prison. It's preparation.

You are not too late. You are dissolving so God can remake you.

And when you're ready—when the cocoon finally cracks—I'll be here, standing in the desert light, cheering for your becoming.

P.S. When you emerge—and you will—come find me. I want to hear your story. I want to witness your becoming. You are not alone.

With love and sovereign grace,
Karen

BONUS SECTION:
RESOURCES FOR YOUR BECOMING

This section is not optional reading. This is your toolkit—the practical resources that turn insight into embodiment, theory into practice, and intention into transformation.

You've read the story. You've received the teaching. Now it's time to do the work.

BONUS SECTION

The 7-Day Embodiment Starter Practice

This is your first week of training for your new life. Each day builds on the last, teaching your body and spirit what it means to be fully present, fully embodied, fully sovereign.

How to use this:

- Start on any day (though starting on a Sunday evening before a new week is ideal)

- Do each practice in order—they build on each other

- Don't rush. Seven days of intentional presence is better than 30 days of distracted going-through-the-motions

- Journal your experience each day. Notice what shifts.

DAY 1: The Body Sanctuary Audit

Purpose: To see clearly—without judgment—how you've been treating your body.

The Practice:

This morning, before you do anything else, sit on the edge of your bed. Place both feet flat on the floor. Close your eyes.

Ask your body these questions, and *listen* for the answers:

1. Where am I holding tension?
    - Scan from head to toe: jaw, shoulders, chest, stomach, lower back, hips, legs
    - Don't try to fix it. Just notice it.

2. When was the last time I felt truly rested?
    - Not "slept," but *rested*—body, mind, and spirit at peace
    - If you can't remember, that's your answer

3. What have I been asking you to do that you don't have the capacity for?
    - Your body will tell you. Maybe it's: "Work 12-hour days." "Skip meals." "Ignore pain." "Carry everyone else's weight."

4. What do you need from me today?

    o The answer might be: Rest. Water. Movement. Stillness. Nourishment. Gentleness.

Journal Prompt: "My body has been trying to tell me _____, but I've been ignoring it because _____. Today, I will honor my body by _____."

The Commitment: Choose ONE thing your body needs today and give it that. Just one.

Maybe it's:
- Drinking 8 glasses of water
- Taking a 20-minute walk
- Going to bed by 10 PM
- Eating a real meal instead of grabbing something quick

One thing. Do it today.

DAY 2: Presence Practice (The 5-Breath Morning)

Purpose: To teach your nervous system that you are no longer in emergency mode.

The Practice:

Tomorrow morning, before you check your phone, before you think about your to-do list, before you respond to anyone else's needs:

1. Sit on the edge of your bed
2. Place both feet flat on the floor
3. Feel the weight of your body (notice how your feet press into the ground, how your body sits on the bed)
4. Take 5 slow breaths:
    - Breathe in for 4 counts
    - Hold for 4 counts
    - Breathe out for 6 counts
    - Repeat 5 times
5. **Say out loud:** "I am present. I am embodied. My body is a temple, and today I will honor it."

Why this works: Your nervous system has been in survival mode for years. It wakes up ready to fight, flee, or freeze. This practice tells your body: "We are safe. The emergency is over. We can be present."

Journal Prompt: "When I took 5 breaths before checking my phone, I noticed _____. My body felt _____. This is different from my usual mornings because _____."

The Commitment: Do this every morning for the next 6 days. Just 2 minutes. That's it.

DAY 3: Rest as Holy (Your First Sabbath Boundary)

Purpose: To practice treating rest as non-negotiable, not as a reward you have to earn.

The Practice:

Today, you're going to set ONE Sabbath boundary—a 24-hour perimeter around a specific time when you will not work, check email, or engage with business.

If you already observe Sabbath (Friday sundown to Saturday sundown), honor it today without guilt or apology.

If you don't observe Sabbath yet, start small: Pick ONE evening this week (tonight, if possible) where you will not work past 6 PM. No email. No "just checking" social media. No "quick" work tasks.

What to do instead:

- Cook a real meal (or order in so you don't have to work)
- Take a bath
- Read something that fills you (Scripture, poetry, a novel)
- Sit outside and watch the sky
- Call someone you love—not to fix them, but just to connect
- Go to bed early

Journal Prompt: "When I stopped working at 6 PM, I felt _____. The hardest part was _____. The most surprising part was _____. Tomorrow, I will honor rest by _____."

The Commitment: This is your first Sabbath boundary. Next week, extend it. Maybe it's two evenings. Then three. Eventually, it becomes your full 24-hour sanctuary.

DAY 4: Weight Release (The 15% Audit)

Purpose: To identify and release ONE unnecessary burden you've been carrying.

The Practice:

You are carrying weight that isn't yours to hold. Today, you're going to identify ONE thing—just one—and release it.

Step 1: The Audit

Make a list of everything you're currently carrying. Not physical items, but *responsibilities, obligations, roles, expectations*.

Examples:
- "I answer my sister's crisis calls at 11 PM"
- "I attend every family gathering even when I'm exhausted"
- "I work on Sundays to 'catch up'"
- "I check work email before bed"
- "I say yes to every request because I'm afraid of disappointing people"

Step 2: The Release

Look at your list. Which ONE item is:
- Not aligned with your season
- Not yours to carry
- Depleting you without serving your purpose
- Something you're doing out of guilt, not calling

Circle it.

Step 3: The Action

Today, you're going to release 15% of that weight. Not all of it—just 15%.

Examples:

- "I will not answer crisis calls after 9 PM. I'll set a boundary."
- "I will skip the next family gathering and rest instead."
- "I will turn off email notifications on Sundays."
- "I will say 'Let me check my calendar and get back to you' instead of auto-yes."

Journal Prompt: "The weight I'm releasing is _____. I've been carrying it because _____. By releasing 15% of this, I'm making space for _____."

The Commitment: This week, release that 15%. Notice how much lighter you feel.

DAY 5: Protective Perimeter (Setting Your First Boundary)

Purpose: To practice protective leadership—guarding what God gave you to steward.

The Practice:

Today, you're going to set ONE boundary that protects your peace.

A boundary is not a wall. A boundary is a *perimeter*—a clear line that says, "This is mine to protect. This does not cross my threshold."

Step 1: Identify What Needs Protection

What is currently violating your peace?

Examples:

- A client who texts you at all hours
- A family member who guilt-trips you
- Social media scrolling that triggers comparison
- Working through meals
- Skipping your morning practice because "there's no time"

Step 2: Set the Boundary

Choose ONE thing. Set a clear boundary around it.

Examples:

- "I will not respond to client texts after 6 PM."
- "I will not engage in guilt-driven conversations. I'll say, 'I understand you're disappointed, but this is my decision.'"

- "I will delete Instagram from my phone for the next 7 days."

- "I will protect my lunch break—30 minutes, no screens, no work."

- "I will not skip my 5-breath morning practice. My peace comes first."

Step 3: Communicate It (If Needed)

If your boundary affects someone else, communicate it clearly:

"I'm setting a new boundary to protect my rest. I won't be responding to texts after 6 PM. If there's an emergency, call me. Otherwise, I'll respond the next morning."

Don't apologize. Don't over-explain. Just state it as fact.

Journal Prompt: "The boundary I set today is _____. I'm protecting my _____. When I set this boundary, I felt _____. The hardest part was _____."

The Commitment: Hold this boundary for the next 7 days. Notice how your peace changes.

DAY 6: Sabbath Preparation (Designing Your Sanctuary Day)

Purpose: To intentionally design what your full Sabbath will look like.

The Practice:

Tomorrow (or the next day you observe Sabbath), you're going to honor a full 24-hour rest. But today, you're going to *prepare* for it.

Why preparation matters: Sabbath is not something you squeeze in after everything else is done. Sabbath is the *foundation* you protect by preparing the other six days around it.

Step 1: Choose Your 24-Hour Window

When will your Sabbath be?

- Biblical Sabbath: Friday sundown to Saturday sundown
- Or another 24-hour window that works for your rhythm

Step 2: Prepare Your Environment

What needs to be handled *before* Sabbath so you can truly rest?

Examples:
- Groceries bought
- Meals prepped (or plan to order in)
- Work projects at a stopping point
- Phone on Do Not Disturb
- Email auto-responder set

Step 3: Design Your Sabbath

What does rest look like for *you*? (Not what you think it "should" look like—what actually fills you.)

Answer these:

- Will I sleep without an alarm?
- Will I cook, or will I order in so I don't work?
- Will I spend time alone, or with loved ones?
- Will I move my body (walk, stretch), or be completely still?
- Will I read, journal, pray, or simply be?
- What will I NOT do? (No email. No work. No social media. No "productivity.")

Step 4: Set the Perimeter

Write down what is *not allowed* to cross your Sabbath boundary:

- Work emails
- Client texts
- Social media scrolling
- House projects
- Guilt about "wasting time"

Journal Prompt: "My Sabbath will be from _____ to _____. During this time, I will _____ and I will NOT _____. I'm protecting this time because _____."

The Commitment: Tomorrow, honor your full 24-hour Sabbath. Don't break it for anyone or anything. Trust that God can hold the world together for 24 hours without you.

DAY 7: Embodied Reflection (Who Are You Becoming?)

Purpose: To witness your own transformation and commit to continuing the practice.

The Practice:

You've completed 6 days of embodiment practice. Today is about reflection and commitment.

Step 1: The Gratitude Scan

Sit quietly. Close your eyes. Place your hand on your heart.

Thank your body for showing up this week:

"Thank you, body, for carrying me through this week. Thank you for teaching me what it means to be present. Thank you for showing me where I've been ignoring you—and for not giving up on me."

Step 2: The Reflection Questions

Journal your answers:

1. **What shifted this week?**
   - How did my body feel different?
   - What did I notice about my energy, my peace, my clarity?

2. **What was hardest?**
   - Which practice challenged me most?
   - What resistance came up?

3. **What surprised me?**
   - What did I learn about myself that I didn't expect?

4. **What do I want to keep?**
   - Which of these 7 practices do I want to make permanent?
   - What would my life look like if I did this every day for a year?

5. **Who am I becoming?**
   - After 7 days of embodiment, who is the woman showing up?
   - What's different about her?

Step 3: The Commitment

Write this out and sign it:

"I commit to embodiment—not as a destination, but as a daily practice. I commit to:

- The 5-breath morning practice (every day)

- One full Sabbath per week (non-negotiable)

- Setting boundaries that protect my peace (as needed)

- Treating my body as a temple (always)

I am no longer 'Survival Me.' I am becoming 'Sovereign Me.' And I will honor her by showing up—imperfect, uncertain, committed—every single day."

Signed: _____ Date: _____

The Commitment: These 7 days were just the beginning. Embodiment is a lifelong practice. Keep going.

Sabbath Business Planning Template

This is your roadmap for designing a business that honors your rest instead of violating it.

The Sabbath-Compatible Business Model

Use this template to audit your current business (or design your new one) through the Sabbath Filter.

The Three Sabbath Filter Questions:

For every offer, every client relationship, every business decision, ask:

1. **Is it emergency-responsive?**

    - Does this require me to be "on call" 24/7?
    - Can this wait until Monday if it comes up on Sabbath?
    - If NO, redesign it or decline it.

2. **Does it respect the weekend?**

    - Does this require Saturday events, Sunday calls, or Friday evening work?
    - Can this be scheduled Monday-Thursday only?
    - If NO, redesign it or decline it.

3. Is it built to honor rest?

    o   Can this offering function while I'm resting?

    o   Does this require my constant presence, or can it be automated/systematized?

    o   If it depletes me, is it sustainable?

    o   If NO, redesign it or decline it.

Your Sabbath-Compatible Week Structure

Design your ideal week with Sabbath as the foundation:

Day	Work Hours	Focus	Sabbath Status
Friday	Until sundown only	Wrap up week, prepare for Sabbath	Sabbath begins at sundown
Saturday	NO WORK	Full Sabbath rest	SACRED—Nothing crosses this boundary
Sunday	After sundown (optional)	Planning for week ahead (if desired)	Sabbath ends at sundown
Monday	4-6 focused hours	Client calls, creation work	Work day
Tuesday	4-6 focused hours	Client calls, content creation	Work day
Wednesday	4-6 focused hours	Admin, emails, planning	Work day
Thursday	4-6 focused hours	Client calls, wrapping up	Work day

Total work hours per week: 20-30 hours

This is *plenty* to build a sustainable, profitable business. You don't need 60-hour weeks. You need focused, intentional hours.

Boundary Scripts for Clients

When you set Sabbath boundaries, you need clear language. Here are scripts you can use:

In Your Client Onboarding:

"I honor Sabbath from Friday sundown through Saturday sundown. During this time, I do not check email, respond to messages, or engage with work. If you send something during Sabbath, I will respond on Sunday evening or Monday morning. Thank you for respecting this boundary."

Your Email Auto-Responder (Sabbath):

"Thank you for your email. I'm currently observing Sabbath rest (Friday sundown - Saturday sundown) and will not be checking messages during this time. I'll respond on [Sunday evening / Monday morning]. If this is a true emergency, please call [emergency contact]. Otherwise, I look forward to connecting with you early next week."

When Someone Asks for a Saturday Call:

"I don't schedule calls on Saturdays as I observe Sabbath rest. I have availability Monday through Thursday. Would one of those days work for you?"

(No apology. No over-explanation. Just clear boundary.)

When Someone Texts You on Sabbath:

Don't respond. Your Sabbath auto-responder should handle it. If they call and it's not an emergency, let it go to voicemail.

If they push back: "I understand this might be inconvenient, but my Sabbath rest is non-negotiable. It's how I'm able to serve you well the other six days. I'll be available again on [day]."

Automation Checklist (So Your Business Runs While You Rest)

Email Automation:

- Welcome sequence for new subscribers (3-5 emails that introduce you and your work)

- Nurture sequence (weekly emails that provide value and build trust)

- Sales sequence for digital products (automated emails that sell your ebook, courses, etc.)

- Sabbath auto-responder (set to activate Friday sundown, deactivate Saturday sundown)

Scheduling Automation:

- Calendly or Acuity (clients can only book during your available hours—Monday-Thursday)

- Buffer zones built in (no back-to-back calls, 15-30 min breaks between)
- No weekend availability showing

Payment Processing:

- Stripe or PayPal for digital products (people can buy 24/7, you get paid automatically)
- Invoicing system for advisory clients (automatic invoices, automatic reminders)

Course/Product Delivery:

- Gumroad, Stan Store, Teachable, or Kajabi (automatic product delivery after purchase)
- No manual fulfillment required

Social Media:

- Posts scheduled in advance (Buffer, Later, or native scheduling)
- DMs can wait until Monday (turn off notifications on Sabbath)

Your 24-Hour Sanctuary Structure

Design your Sabbath with intentionality:

Hour 0 (Friday Sundown - The Closing):
- Light a candle
- Close your laptop
- Turn off work notifications
- Say a prayer: "This is the day the Lord has made. I will rest in it."

Hours 1-12 (Deep Rest):
- Sleep without an alarm
- Wake naturally
- Slow breakfast
- No email, no news, no social media
- Read, pray, sit in silence

Hours 13-24 (Soul Feed):
- Walk outside
- Connect with loved ones
- Cook a special meal (or order in)
- Read Scripture or something that fills you
- Journal, create, rest

Hour 24 (Saturday Sundown - The Opening):
- Light a candle
- Give thanks for rest
- Transition back into the week with clarity and peace

BONUS SECTION

Scripture Study Guide: Embodiment, Rest & Sovereignty

Use this guide for personal study or small group discussion.

FOR EMBODIMENT (Your Body as Temple)

"Do you not know that your bodies are temples of the Holy Spirit, who is in you, whom you have received from God? You are not your own; you were bought at a price. Therefore honor God with your bodies." -1 Corinthians 6:19-20

Reflection Questions:

- How have I been treating my body—as a temple or as a tool?

- What does it mean to "honor God" with my body?

- What would change if I truly believed my body was a sacred dwelling place?

_____

_____

_____

"Be still, and know that I am God." - Psalm 46:10

Reflection Questions:

- When was the last time I was truly *still*—not just physically, but mentally and spiritually?

_____

_____

_____

- What am I afraid will happen if I stop moving, stop doing, stop performing?

_____

_____

_____

- How does stillness help me know God?

"I praise you because I am fearfully and wonderfully made; your works are wonderful, I know that full well." - Psalm 139:14

Reflection Questions:

- Do I believe my body—scarred, tired, imperfect as it is—is "wonderfully made"?

- What would it look like to praise God *for* my body instead of apologizing for it?

- How can I honor the body God gave me today?

FOR REST/SABBATH (Rest as Holy)

Exodus 20:8-10 *"Remember the Sabbath day by keeping it holy. Six days you shall labor and do all your work, but the seventh day is a sabbath to the Lord your God. On it you shall not do any work."*

Reflection Questions:

- Am I *remembering* Sabbath, or am I treating it as optional?

_____

_____

_____

- What does it mean to keep a day "holy"—set apart, sacred, protected?

_____

_____

_____

- What "work" am I still doing on my Sabbath that I need to release?

_____

_____

_____

"Then, because so many people were coming and going that they did not even have a chance to eat, he said to them, 'Come with me by yourselves to a quiet place and get some rest.'" - **Mark 6:31**

Reflection Questions:

- Jesus withdrew to rest even when people still needed Him. Why do I think I don't have that same permission?

- What is my "quiet place"—where do I go to truly rest?

- What would it look like to withdraw *before* I'm completely depleted?

"The Lord is my shepherd, I lack nothing. He makes me lie down in green pastures, he leads me beside quiet waters, he refreshes my soul." ~ **Psalm 23:1-3**

Reflection Questions:

- God *makes* the sheep lie down. Why? Because sheep won't rest on their own. Am I the same?

_____

_____

_____

- When was the last time I felt my soul was truly *refreshed*?

_____

_____

_____

- What "green pastures" and "quiet waters" is God inviting me to?

_____

_____

_____

"Come to me, all you who are weary and burdened, and I will give you rest. Take my yoke upon you and learn from me, for I am gentle and humble in heart, and you will find rest for your souls. For my yoke is easy and my burden is light." - **Matthew 11:28-30**

Reflection Questions:

- Jesus offers rest, yet I'm exhausted. What burden am I carrying that He never asked me to carry?

- What does it mean that His "yoke is easy" and His "burden is light"? How is mine different?

- What would it look like to actually accept His offer of rest?

FOR BECOMING/TRANSFORMATION (Metamorphosis)

"Therefore, if anyone is in Christ, the new creation has come: The old has gone, the new is here!" ~**2 Corinthians 5:17**

Reflection Questions:

- What "old" am I still clinging to that God is asking me to release?

- Do I believe I can truly be a "new creation," or do I think my past defines me forever?

- What does the "new" look like for me?

"Do not conform to the pattern of this world, but be transformed by the renewing of your mind. Then you will be able to test and approve what God's will is—his good, pleasing and perfect will." - **Romans 12:2**

Reflection Questions:

- What "patterns of this world" have I been conforming to? (Hustle culture? Performance? Depletion?)

_____

_____

_____

- What does "renewing of your mind" look like in practice?

_____

_____

_____

- How will I know God's will if my mind is still filled with the world's expectations?

_____

_____

_____

"Forget the former things; do not dwell on the past. See, I am doing a new thing! Now it springs up; do you not perceive it? I am making a way in the wilderness and streams in the wasteland." - **Isaiah 43:18-19**

Reflection Questions:

- What "former things" do I need to stop dwelling on?

- Do I believe God is doing a "new thing" in my life right now, or do I think my season of becoming has passed?

- Where is God making "a way in the wilderness" for me?

"Being confident of this, that he who began a good work in you will carry it on to completion until the day of Christ Jesus." - **Philippians 1:6**

Reflection Questions:

- God started this work in me. Do I trust Him to complete it?

_____

_____

_____

- What "good work" has God begun in me that I've been too impatient to see through?

_____

_____

_____

- How does this promise give me grace for the messy middle?

_____

_____

_____

FOR SOVEREIGNTY/STRENGTH (You Are Clothed in Strength and Dignity)

*"She sets about her work vigorously; her arms are strong for her tasks." - **Proverbs 31:17***

Reflection Questions:

- The Proverbs 31 woman's arms were strong—not from depletion, but from stewardship. How can I build strength without sacrificing my body?

_____

_____

_____

- What does "vigorous" work look like when it's built on a foundation of rest?

_____

_____

_____

- Am I confusing exhaustion with strength?

_____

_____

_____

"She is clothed with strength and dignity; she can laugh at the days to come." - **Proverbs 31:25**

Reflection Questions:

- Am I clothed in strength and dignity, or am I clothed in exhaustion and anxiety?

- What would it look like to "laugh at the days to come" instead of fearing them?

- What do I need to release to step into this kind of sovereignty?

"But those who hope in the Lord will renew their strength. They will soar on wings like eagles; they will run and not grow weary, they will walk and not be faint." - **Isaiah 40:31**

Reflection Questions:

- I've been running and growing weary. What does it mean to "hope in the Lord" in a way that actually renews my strength?

_____
_____
_____

- What would it look like to "soar" instead of survive?

_____
_____
_____

- Do I believe this promise applies to me at my age, in my season?

_____
_____
_____

"Now to him who is able to do immeasurably more than all we ask or imagine, according to his power that is at work within us."
- **Ephesians 3:20**

Reflection Questions:

- Do I believe God can do "immeasurably more" than I imagine—or have I settled for survival?

- What am I asking for that's too small?

- What does it mean that His power is "at work within" me right now?

The Sovereign Soft Life Reading & Resource List

These are books, teachers, and resources that align with the work of embodiment, Kingdom business, and Sabbath living.

Books on Embodiment & Healing

"Healing Whispers: A 31-Day Faith Journey to Overcome Toxic Motherhood and Reclaim Your Power" by Karen Y. Moore

- A 31-day devotional for women healing from the wounds of toxic motherhood—whether you experienced it or perpetuated it. This is where I first began teaching what it means to break generational cycles and reclaim your sovereignty.

"Healing Whispers: Empowerment Through Color. Resilience Warriors Edition" by Karen Y. Moore

- A companion journal and coloring book for women processing trauma, grief, and the journey toward wholeness.

"The Body Keeps the Score" by Bessel van der Kolk

- For understanding how trauma lives in your body and how to release it

"When the Body Says No" by Gabor Maté

- On the cost of hidden stress and how your body forces you to listen

"Burnout: The Secret to Unlocking the Stress Cycle" by Emily Nagoski & Amelia Nagoski

- Practical strategies for completing the stress cycle (essential for caregivers and high-performers)

"Daring Greatly" by Brené Brown

- On vulnerability, shame, and showing up as your whole self

Books on Sabbath & Rest

"The Rest of God" by Mark Buchanan

- A theological and practical look at Sabbath rest

"Sabbath as Resistance" by Walter Brueggemann

- Sabbath as an act of defiance against the culture of productivity

"Sacred Rest" by Dr. Saundra Dalton-Smith

- The seven types of rest you need (not just physical sleep)

"24/6: The Power of Unplugging One Day a Week" by Tiffany Shlain

- A secular but practical take on the power of a full day offline

Books on Kingdom Business & Stewardship

"Business for the Glory of God" by Wayne Grudem

- How business, when done with integrity, glorifies God

"Your Money or Your Life" by Vicki Robin

- Transforming your relationship with money and achieving financial independence

"The 4-Hour Workweek" by Tim Ferriss

- Not about laziness, but about designing a business that doesn't consume your life

"Essentialism" by Greg McKeown

- The disciplined pursuit of less—doing fewer things, but better

Podcasts & Teachers

"The Rose-Minded Podcast" by Carly Kocurek

- Faith, business, and building with intention

"That Sounds Fun with Annie F. Downs"

- Joy, faith, and living well

"The Happy Hour with Jamie Ivey"

- Conversations with women of faith about real life

"Online Marketing Made Easy with Amy Porterfield"

- Practical business-building strategies (filter through your Sabbath lens)

For Sepsis Survivors

Sepsis Alliance

- Website: www.sepsis.org
- Resources, support groups, and education for survivors

CDC Sepsis Information

- Website: www.cdc.gov/sepsis
- Medical information and warning signs

How to Work With Karen

If you're ready to take the next step in your becoming, here's how we can work together.

Private Advisory

For the woman ready for high-level, one-on-one support.

This is for you if:

- You're navigating reinvention after loss, caregiving, or trauma
- You're building a Kingdom business and need strategic guidance
- You're transitioning from depletion to embodied sovereignty
- You want someone in your corner who understands what you've survived

What we'll work on together:

- Your business model (Sabbath-compatible, revenue-generating, sustainable)
- Your embodiment practice (body as temple, not tool)
- Your boundaries and protective perimeter

- Your Sabbath architecture

- Your marketing and messaging (from embodied authority, not hustle)

- Your legacy vision (what you're building for the next 10-20 years)

Structure:

- 3-6 month engagements

- Scheduled calls (your schedule, Monday-Thursday only)

- Voxer support between calls

- Strategic planning and accountability

Capacity: 3-5 clients at a time (so I can be fully present with you)

Next Steps: Visit karenymoore.com for application details and availability.

"The Sovereign Soft Life" Cohort

For the woman ready for group transformation.

This is for you if:

- You're done performing strength and ready to embody sovereignty
- You want to build a business that honors your Sabbath
- You're tired of hustle culture and ready for Kingdom alignment
- You want a sisterhood of women who are also choosing themselves

What we'll cover:

- Embodiment practices (moving from survival to sovereignty)
- Sabbath as architecture (designing your week around rest)
- Removing unnecessary weight (the 15% release practice)
- Building your business model (Sabbath-compatible revenue streams)
- Setting boundaries without guilt
- The Proverbs 31 woman reimagined

Structure:

- 6-8 weeks
- Weekly 90-minute group calls (Monday-Thursday evenings)
- Community support between calls

- Workbooks and reflection guides
- Guest teachers on specialized topics

Next cohort: Q2 2026

Next Steps: Visit karenymoore.com to join the waitlist.

Quarterly Masterclasses

For the woman ready for focused, deep-dive teaching.

Topics:

- "Embodied Faith: Your Body as Temple"
- "The Proverbs 31 Blueprint for Modern Women"
- "Building the Sovereign Soft Life"
- "Sabbath Business Planning"

Structure:

- 90 minutes live (teaching + Q&A)
- Recorded and available as replay
- Actionable workbook included
- Held on Saturday afternoons (after Sabbath ends)

Next masterclass: Details at karenymoore.com

The Becoming Her Collective

For the woman ready for ongoing community and support.

This is a sacred gathering of women walking the path of embodiment, sovereignty, and Kingdom business building.

What's included:

- Monthly live teachings
- Weekly embodiment practices
- Community forum for connection and support
- Resource library (guides, templates, frameworks)
- Guest experts on specialized topics
- Early access to new offerings

Launching: Within 3-6 months

Next Steps: Join the waitlist at karenymoore.com

Speaking & Teaching

For churches, women's conferences, and faith-based business events.

Topics I speak on:

- Embodiment and the Sovereign Soft Life
- The Proverbs 31 Woman Reimagined
- From Survival to Sovereignty
- Sabbath-Honoring Business Building
- Choosing Yourself Without Abandoning Your Faith
- The Second Act: Becoming After 50

Format: Keynotes, workshops, panel discussions

Availability: Limited dates (to protect my Sabbath and my own becoming)

Booking inquiries: karenymoore.com/speaking

Stay Connected

Website: www.karenymoore.com

- Weekly essays on embodiment, sovereignty, and the Sovereign Soft Life
- Frameworks and reflections
- Updates on new offerings

Instagram: @kymlifestyle LinkedIn: Karen Y. Moore

I post 3x per week:

- Monday: Faith/Scripture on embodiment and rest
- Wednesday: Lessons from my journey
- Friday: Business wisdom and Sabbath-honoring strategies

If you want to walk this path with me, that's where I'll be showing up—raw, real, and committed to the becoming.

You are not alone in your emergence. Come build the Sovereign Soft Life with me.

YOUR NEXT STEPS

You've finished the book. But your becoming is just beginning.

Here's how to continue:

1. Start the 7-Day Embodiment Practice (Bonus Section, Page X)

2. Join the waitlist for The Becoming Her Collective

3. Connect with Karen at www.karenymoore.com

Share this book with one woman who needs to hear: "You are not too late. You are exactly on time."

Use #BecomingHer to share your journey.

ABOUT THE AUTHOR

Karen Y. Moore is a faith-based embodiment coach, advisor, and author helping women build modern-day Proverbs 31 lives—strong, sovereign, and rooted in rest, not exhaustion.

After sixteen years as a caregiver, surviving sepsis three times, and losing her husband to the same illness, Karen chose herself at 57. She made what she calls "the Sacred Exit"—leaving Savannah for Las Vegas, where she now teaches women how to embody their sovereignty and build Kingdom businesses that honor the Sabbath.

A graduate of the Institute for Integrative Nutrition and a certified Christian life coach, Karen brings over 25 years of luxury hospitality experience into her advisory work. She is the author of "Healing Whispers: A 31-Day Faith Journey to Overcome Toxic Motherhood and Reclaim Your Power" and co-author of the upcoming "I Have Found The One Whom My Soul Loves: Two Love Stories, One Standard" with Sonya Snow, MA, LPC, CCTP."

Karen lives in Las Vegas, Nevada, where she is building the Sovereign Soft Life—and inviting other women to join her.

Connect with her at www.karenymoore.com

Instagram: @kymlifestyle | LinkedIn: Karen Y. Moore

www.ingramcontent.com/pod-product-compliance
Lightning Source LLC
LaVergne TN
LVHW021657060526
838200LV00050B/2386